I0109001

Photo by Laura Burke

ABOUT THE AUTHOR

Angela Shelton is a screenwriter, author and actress. Her first novel was adapted into the movie *Tumbleweeds in 2000.* She won a regional Emmy in 2005 for her portrayal of Safe Side Superchick in the series created by Baby Einstein's Julie Clark. The do-gooder Angela spent almost a decade traveling the country encouraging people to stop raping each other. She now splits her time between LA and New York. She has been eating well recently and writing a series of children's books.

Will Date 4 Food

PRAISE FOR
WILL DATE 4 FOOD

"Angela Shelton is a hilarious, insightful and soulful comic force. Her life experiences and lyrical philosophies make for a great read in lean times."

Rick Overton
Screenwriter, Actor, and Comedian

"In Will Date 4 Food, Angela Shelton shows you how to cast a wide net with a dose of humor while looking for conversation, a pleasant meal, and even love online."

Julie Spira

Online dating expert and bestselling author
The Perils of Cyber-Dating: Confessions of a Hopeful Romantic Looking for Love Online.

"BRAVO! Angela does it again. With her usual humor and irony, Angela gives women a how-to book on dating and eating at the same time. Teaching women how to fish for food while meeting interesting men is cyber-GENIUS."

Rhonda Dean
Victim Advocate

*"Brilliant and healthy guide to online dating! Just think~ **Will Date 4 Food** can give you years of healthy living if you let other people pay for your expensive organic meals. I condone this behavior and guide not only for amusement but for economical and physical health. Finally making online dating less shudderific, and more entertabulous! Plus, you'll become a well-fed, better listener as a result."*

Lindsay Eberts
Holistic Health Counselor
Lindsayskitchenworkshop.com

Will Date 4 Food offers a liberating approach to the ever so daunting world of online dating, with essential and simple do and do not(s). While Angela's courage is as infectious as always, her wisdom invites us to enjoy our breakfast, lunch and dinner and not to take ourselves too seriously.

Katharine Blodget
Masters in Social Work(MSW)
and Behavior Analyst

(AN ONLINE DATING GUIDE FOR GIRLS WHO CAN'T AFFORD TO EAT OUT)

WRITTEN BY ANGELA SHELTON

Published by Quiet Owl Books

WILL DATE 4 FOOD
(AN ONLINE DATING GUIDE FOR GIRLS WHO CAN'T AFFORD TO EAT OUT)

Cover Design by Jennifer Welker

Set in 12-point Palatino

First Quiet Owl Books paperback edition 2011
ISBN-13: 978-0615548913
ISBN-10: 0615548911

Published by Quiet Owl Books
quietowl.com

Quiet Owl Books are available for bulk purchases in the US at special discounts. For more information please contact the Special Markets Department at sales@quietowl.com.

Dedicated to all the hungry girls and women who have gone into debt supporting starving artist boyfriends, deadbeat husbands, miscellaneous family members, and who still insist on picking up the check or going Dutch.

Ladies, it's time for you to eat.

Will Date 4 Food

TABLE OF CONTENTS

FORWARD
BY WENDY MURPHY

If you've ever paid the bill at a restaurant, not only for your own meal but also for your date's, and sometimes for everyone else at the table, too, or if you've ever insisted that you should "take care" of things while those around you sit idly by and take advantage of your generous personality, this book will change your life.

Angela Shelton gives you all the tools you need to break free from the habits that ruined your finances, turned you into a sucker and propelled you to date all the hangers-on who dragged you down into a pit of poverty and self-pity.

Too many women waste time, in the real world and on-line, looking for "Prince Charming". They don't dedicate nearly enough energy thinking about their own needs and noticing that Prince Charming is actually a slob or a leech.

Will Date 4 Food is a perfect antidote to this craziness. Filled with serious advice, funny stories and even a few good recipes, this book will take you from your laptop to a great dinner with an interesting guy in record time.

Better yet, this book will transform you from a person who puts herself second, third - or last - to a woman who realizes her value and puts herself first for a change. Just sit back and enjoy the ride when all sorts of wonderful things, start landing in your lap when you're not even trying.

One minute you're learning about online dating, and before you know it, you're figuring out your finances, listening to people around you with a whole new perspective, and literally eating healthy food while spending time with really nice, interesting guys!

This liberating, frolic of a read is going to lift your spirits and fill your bank account while loading you up with real nutrition, paid for by the kinds of men who want to feed you because they find you are utterly delightful!

As it should be.

Wendy Murphy
JD Law Professor, Women's Advocate
and Author of *And Justice For Some*
seen on NBC, MSNBC, CNN, CNBC, Fox News
The O'Reilly Factor and Nancy Grace

INTRODUCTION
OR
WHY IN THE WORLD TO DATE FOR FOOD

Have you ever been broke? The truth of the matter is that most of us have experienced hard times and we all need to eat. I love food. I love going out to eat. I love fine dining. I love diners. I love drive-ins. I love eating, period. But I, like many of my friends who were not trained in the art of finances or love, was broke when I started this project. I barely had the money to eat at home, much less eating out, which is one of my favorite things to do in life!

I also had a history of picking up the check, paying for men, supporting starving artists, giving friends money, and making sure everyone's needs were met, all while forgetting to save for a rainy day myself.

When my girlfriends began to tell me how they were online dating, I scoffed at the thought. I had been single for quite some time and saw no need, nor resources, for a boyfriend.

But when my friends told me about all the dinners they were going on, my interest was piqued. When my friend Gloria *(I changed her name to keep her dating secretes private)* told me about all the dinners she was having each week and how she wasn't romantically involved with any of the men, I was in. I decided to date for food and break my pattern of always picking up the check.

I know you have the same problem; otherwise you would not be checking out this book. You see the "potential" in that starving artist boyfriend who doesn't do laundry. You hear the future rock star in that out-of-work waiter and see maybe husband material in that male model. Please smack yourself in the head. Better yet, just keep reading. You are not alone!

There are many of us out there who have made these mistakes. And yes, many of those boyfriends, the ones with the bongs and no jobs, that you fed with your hard earned money, went on to be rich and famous.

If not, your past mooches went and got a job after you finally stopped paying for their pizza. But are they sending you dividends and profit sharing checks? I didn't think so. Did they even so much as pay back what they put on your credit card or stole from your secret cash stash? Of course not. Do you still scoff at the idea of letting the man picking up the check? Is it because you're trying to prove that you're a generous and capable gal? You're about to change your ways.

It's time to stop your nonsense. I did and I'm going to show you how to do it too. I've been there. I've made the same mistakes. Then I got the bills.

But if you're like me, which would make you awesome, you know that it's the awesome women who tend to take care of everyone else but themselves. I'm here to tell you that you can still be your adorable awesome and keep your money in your own wallet!

Dating for food removes expectations of love, romance, and trying to find the "man of your dreams." It opens up new kinds of dialogues with very cool men you may never have met if you had not shared a meal with them (and let them pay). Strangely enough, by dating for food instead of trying to find Prince Charming, I actually made great friends for life, including men I introduced to girlfriends, and a few I even got to work for me on various projects. Not only is dating for food good for nutrition, it's good for business! You entrepreneur cougars like hearing that, don't you?

I found a cameraman, editor, graphic designer, animator, and a photographer from online dating. I also met an honest to goodness boyfriend unexpectedly, but you'll read about that. I'll spare you the details since this is about food, not romance! But when a good meal is the goal, exciting things can happen; things you don't plan for and may never expect. It's what happens when you open your mind (and mouth) to a whole new purpose of dating.

Whether dating for food helps you find a new job, a new friend or gets you nothing more than a belly full of something delicious, this book will bring you rewards you've never dreamed of - and best of all - it will save you tons of money.

Let's get started already, you're hungry.

CHAPTER 1

DIVING INTO CYBERSPACE

GET STARTED, YOU'RE HUNGRY!

The goal of *Will Date 4 Food* is to not spend any money except of course for gas, because there's no way you are going to let anyone pick you up at your house. Why? Because then they will know where you live! Duh. I searched through all of the online dating sites I could find, and they were so expensive that I was almost derailed before I even began. If I had the money to pay for all the online dating charges, I'd take myself out for dinner!

Do Not Let Your Date Pick You Up!

The only site I found that was free and decent was **Nerve.com.**

I'm sure there are other dating sites out there that are free and great too. When you find them, please post in the comments section on **WillDate4Food.com**.

I thought Nerve was fitting because it takes some nerve to date for food so that's the site I picked.   Many online romance coaches suggest that you sign up for multiple sites so I tried that at first. I found some that claim to match people to millionaires and "wealthy men", but they seriously grossed me out. I even put up a profile for a short time on a few of those sites, but so many freaks and weirdoes contacted me that I shut them all down. Any site can have weirdoes, but Nerve.com worked the best for me.   Plus, Nerve's database is the same as the Onion Personals and the "Onion" is funny. Funny is good.

Go to www.nerve.com and click on "Nerve Personals" on the upper left corner. Don't let the look of the site scare you. I thought it was a horn-dog site at first too.

But the site is harmless and pretty cool and it worked so try it!

Choose "Join Now" and create a username and password. Don't be scared. This chapter is not called *Diving into Cyberspace* for nothing!

Everyone can see the username you pick so choose one that stands out well. I used SouthernerinLA and FeedaFox. I recommend not using anything sexual like HorneyHotLips or TastyTonight.

Be tasteful but clever. I was walking the line with FeedaFox. I'll get more into your full profile later in Chapter 4 – *What's on Your Hook?*

The site ads are true - it is free. It only

Do Not Upgrade Your Account!

costs money to upgrade to the silver or gold memberships but you're not allowed to do that if you're following the **Date 4 Food Rules** (coming up in Chapter 2).

Remember, you are not going to spend any money!

After you sign up you will receive an email to activate your account. The site will try again to get you to upgrade you're account but don't you dare do it! There will also be some sexy pictures on the site but don't be afraid. The personals are not part of a sex site (unless your username is SluttySally).

Every dating site will then bombard you with notices about who is checking you out and how you should upgrade to find your man. I don't care how many times your dating site of choice sends you email offers to upgrade – do not upgrade! You are not spending any money on dating and the upgrades are usually a whopping $19 bucks a month. You could buy Tupperware for your leftovers with that money. Think about your future!

Don't start looking at men until you fill out your basic profile. Calm down, Cougar.

In the top left corner of the site you will see Home, an icon of an envelope (that is where your future dinner invites will show up) and My Account. Click on "My Account." In the box to the left you will see your basic profile, personal info, stats, physical info, photos and video, additional details, location and personality quiz. Fill out your basic profile information first.

Here is where you choose what you're looking for from the age and height to the hair and eye color of your date.

The choices are: Man, Woman, Couple (man and woman), Couple (2 women), or Couple (2 men) for Casual dating, Serious Relationship, Friendship, Activity Partners or Play. Go ahead and choose. Your stomach is growling.

"Couples" Are Not Looking to Share a Meal.

I am mainly writing to women who are going out with men, but if going out with women is your thing, then by all means choose women. But be warned that you will probably end up going Dutch most of the time and miss some free meals going down that path. Sorry but that's just the way it is with lesbians on these sites. They're so damn egalitarian; you'll never eat for free! I know you're fed up with men but there's no need to rent a U-Haul, move in with a lesbian lover and split all the bills just yet.

There's no need to give up on dating men for food just because you're a lesbian either. Gay or not, if you want to eat for free, choose men for casual dating, serious relationship, friendship, activity partners or play. The only guys you should stay away from are the ones hoping to date you as part of a couple. If you're really interested in food, don't agree to "date" a couple. There's a good chance they're not looking for dinner guests.

I recommend choosing men for casual dating, serious relationship, friendship, activity partners or play. Select them all! I know we're talking about searching for food here but while trying get your belly filled, it is possible you might just meet the love of your life. That's why you have to check off "serious relationship" in your profile when you say what you're looking for. Plus, a very cool guy could want to feed you AND start something serious, and if you didn't select it, you won't show up in his search results, which means you'd miss out on a good meal as well as a good romance.

CHAPTER 2
THE RULES

YOU MUST FOLLOW THESE

Before we go any further you need to know the rules. I put a one page summary at the back of the book so you can just rip them out and keep them with you at all times. (Please buy the book first, before you do any ripping) If your phone has a camera, snap a picture of the Rules and refer to them whenever you need advice.

Share this on Facebook.

Put the Rules on your Facebook wall. Tag Facebook.com/willdateforfood as well as /angelasheltonfanpage. Of course if you share this on Facebook, don't be an idiot and friend your dates! If you do put them under "restricted" so they don't see that you're Dating 4 Food for crying out loud.

RULES FOR WILL DATE 4 FOOD!

RULE NUMBER 1: Never have anyone pick you up at your house. Meet your dates at a mutually agreeable establishment. More than everything else, you need to be safe which means not letting your date know where you live.

RULE NUMBER 2: Have a Dating Buddy aka the Gay Mafia. This is who knows where you're going and whom you are going out with and even better than that, drops you off and picks you up.

RULE NUMBER 3: Do not meet for drinks or coffee. The whole point is to eat real food not bar snacks.

RULE NUMBER 4: Do not focus on romance. Focus on the food. (If love shows up, that's a great extra helping, not the goal.)

RULE NUMBER 5: Do not upgrade your online dating account or spend any money on dating sites.

RULE NUMBER 6: Do not pick up the check (duh) even to "go Dutch". You are not allowed to pay. Remember, you're dating for food.

RULE NUMBER 7: Listen Listen Listen. Let him talk while you eat. Bet you never did that before.

RULE NUMBER 8: Go out with anyone who asks (minus weirdoes, freaks and creeps).

RULE NUMBER 9: Check your issues with the valet and hold your tongue. This is no time to treat your date like he's your therapist. You can't have a free mean and a free counseling session.

RULE NUMBER 10: Eat Well. Do not order just a salad. Go for sustenance.

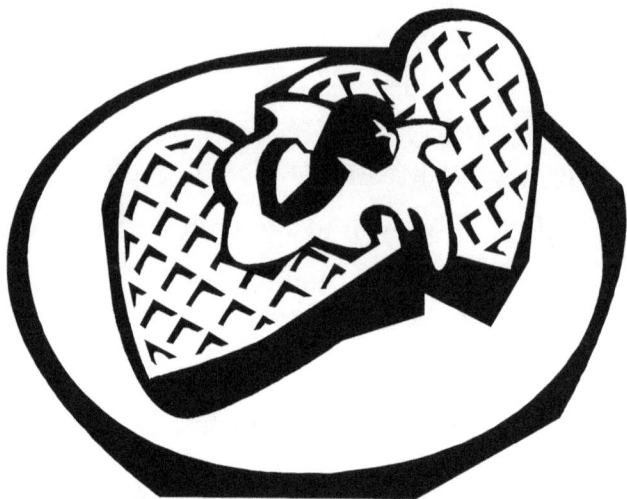

Chapter 3

YOUR DATING BUDDY
AKA THE GAY MAFIA

If you don't have a gay best friend, I pity you. I really do. Every girl needs a gay best friend. Get one. Or borrow your best friend's gay best friend. If you really don't have one, go hang out in West Hollywood or wherever the cool kids hang out in your town and make friends. Your gay best friend can save your life.

Get Yourself a Gay Best Friend!

Why does my dating buddy have to be gay, you ask? Because he will protect you like no other knight in the world will. It's true. Your girlfriends can come with you on your dates or wait in the car, but unless you have a martial arts expert as a gal-pal, or the girl who insisted on playing in the male football league in high school, they are not going to have the same affect as an angry gay guy.

If you've never seen a gay guy be protective, you are missing out. Mine actually pulled an axe out and held it over his head as he warned my date that he was watching everything he did. Seriously. We both thought the date was a little weird so we had to come up with something even weirder to keep they guy in check. As predicted, the weirdo didn't try anything weird with me. He didn't dare because he knew my gay best friend was outside with an axe! Best of all, the weirdo figured out quickly that he wasn't going to try anything funky with me - so the date ended fast and I took home lots of great leftovers!

Of course, there's a catch with leftovers – you should share them with your other girlfriends who are *Dating for Food* and of course your Gay Best Friend!

Skip ahead to Chapter 14 – *Will Date 4 Food Recipes* to find out how to stretch a meal. Team up with your girlfriends who are **Dating for Food** and share leftovers. There are many bonuses to having a gay best friend, besides being protected.

He will help you with things like picking out the right outfit and, and making sure your hair and make-up looks spectacular. He will make sure you don't look too slutty or too much like a teenager, (which are often the same thing). He will be honest with you if you have something green in your teeth and if your hair looks too puffy or too flat.

He will get a kick out of the fact that you are **Dating 4 Food**, but he will probably give you hell for **Rule Number 8** – which requires that you go out with anyone who asks (minus weirdoes, freaks and creeps). He will tell you not to lower your standards, for example, when he sees that you're meeting a guy nicknamed "Mr. Chubb".

This is when you remind him that you are dating for *food.* Tell him to suck it and focus on how yummy his share of the leftovers will be when you skedaddle out of there faster than he can organize his organza scarves. Trust me. He will love you for sticking it out with "Mr. Chubb" the minute he sees you making one of the *Recipes for Leftovers.*

If he still gives you hell, buy him an "I Suck" T-shirt. He will get the joke and wear it and who knows, you may help him meet a "friend" too and get more than just food from dating.

Tight fitted T's are a small price to pay for keeping your gay best friend happy. You can get them at **cafepress.com/imateasets** aka *I'm a Tease T's.* That was my gay best friend's idea. While you're at it, visit the *WillDate4Food* store at cafepress.com/willdate4food and get a ***Will Date 4 Food*** T-shirt. Let people know you're hungry.

When you use the money you're saving on dating to buy a T-shirt there, I a few bucks too. Lord knows I could use it! I have to eat too, you know.

All kidding aside, you need some kind of code word or *a certain look* to communicate with your dating buddy. If you're on a date with a weirdo, freak or creep, your dating buddy needs to get in there and save you. More on this in Chapter 17 – *Weirdoes, Freaks & Creeps,* but I want to emphasize safety and remind you that you need your dating partner to be as wild as mine was.

If your favorite member of the Gay Mafia needs to hold an axe above his head and threaten that no man has seen the fury of an angry gay man, let him do it. If your gay best friend can think of another way to threaten a weirdo, go for it. Don't hurt anyone needlessly, but make it very clear that things will get ugly if any weirdo does anything except enjoy your lovely company.

If your dating buddy does a good job, and keeps you safe from harm during a date with a weirdo, get him a gift card to Home Depot (or some home decorating place he likes) so he knows you value his help. This is of course after the "I Suck" T-shirt. If he's got a fitted T and a gift card, you can be sure you can call upon him at any time. Keep him happy.

Believe me, bringing along a straight male, as your dating buddy does not work. Not only is it a threat to your date and kind of disrespectful, it just doesn't work.

Don't Bring Your Straight Buddy on Your Date!

The straight men tend to miss any sign of an actual problem while your gay buddy can spot a weirdo from a block away. If there is a problem with a date, your straight buddy may actually get into an altercation, which is not necessary.

Your gay buddy will just scare your date away. If you need a good escape route, your gay best friend is the way to go! Again, if you don't have one, go get one. There is no safer place than within the arms of the Gay Mafia. Befriend them today.

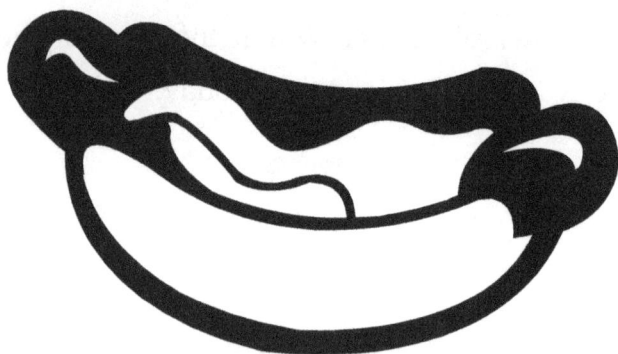

CHAPTER 4

WHAT'S ON YOUR HOOK?

WHAT'S YOUR HEADLINE?

Before you start dating, you have to set up a profile. This is the sales pitch you write about yourself. It allows the guys scrolling through the pages of ladies to be able to spot you. The first thing that grabs their attention is your headline.

Your Headline and Your Picture are Your Bait!

I already warned you to not choose a headline that was too slutty. Now, I want you to choose some more. You don't want just one. Headlines are like advertising. Some ads make some people buy and others make them scroll right past.

A guy might stop and read your whole profile if your headline makes him laugh and another guy might ask you out if your headline made him think of home.

One of my most popular headlines was SouthernerinLA. I had my share of BBQ dates! Your headline does not need to summarize your full personality. All you're trying to do is get a guy to stop and check out your profile instead of someone else's. It helps to have a great photo, too. We'll get to the pictures in a moment but let's focus on your headline first. Choose a few of them and change them up to see which one gets the most bites.

I used Southerner in LA and Feed a Fox. I swapped those out with others like:

To Feed Me or Not to Feed Me

Hungry Heroes

No Nuts Please

Hungry Girl in LA

Be clever but to the point. Again, I suggest shying away from anything sexual like "I like to eat nuts" because you will be solicited by some real whackos. I was walking the line with "Feed a Fox" and "No Nuts Please".

Think of your headline kind of like the way you think about what you wear when you go to a bar. If you dress in a super sexy, bimbo way, you will attract a certain kind of guy, but if you dress to express yourself as a person who is funny, classy and clever, you are more likely to attract guys who genuinely like funny and clever women. These are exactly the kind of men who will want to feed you simply because they enjoy your funny, clever company! Remember, you're out to get food, so think about your headline not as bait for any old date, but bait for a guy who is likely to appreciate your need for belly-filling sustenance.

The only exception is that you should avoid the creeps and wackos. Nobody is worth your time, even for a good meal, if they're truly creepy.

Keep Reading.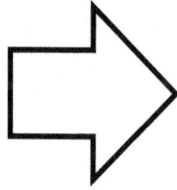

Your ABOUT ME Section

Here comes the part where you talk about yourself in the "About Me" section. Be honest, funny, and as clever as you can. People get a kick out of profiles and it can and will lead to food.

Here's my profile. Feel free to re-use any part of it for your own profile. I like to share.

Reuse Anything In My Profile for Your Own!

FEED A FOX

I've been told that I'm funny, talented, crazy, tall, courageous, hot and the ugliest pretty girl with goofy faces. I've also been told that I'm a workaholic with very bad A.D.D. but I am not sure I believe in all that nonsense. What about good old-fashioned energetic creativity? I am busy doing fun things in the world but I always have time for a good meal and conversation.

Starting dance floors is my most favorite thing in the whole world to do. I love live music, events, theater, traveling, motorcycle rides, hikes, bike rides and food. I go on bike rides and hikes daily. I eat organic as much as I but can't resist Ben and Jerry's Chubby Hubby. I tried to be a vegan but I'm Southern and I failed. I like ribs.

The idea of online dating for the sake of hooking up makes me want to vomit. I am not seeking a man for the sake of hunting for love and affection. I am on here because I'm interested in meeting cool people and so far I have met some awesome people.

I don't have the ability to message you or wink. Winking, much like flirting, costs money and I'm into saving all I can after supporting a slew of starving artists. But I can and I will add you to my hotlist if I think you're interesting. So hit me up and let's share a meal. Hope you're having a great day.

Notice I talked a tiny bit about saving money but did not go on and on about how that deadbeat ex of mine stole my computer and lost my dog. I also showed that I had a sense of humor and was not looking for a hook up. Don't go into a whole lot of detail about all the things you don't want. Be sweet, short and funny as much as possible.

Be Sweet, To the Point and Funny.

Since you signed up for the free standard profile and are not going to spend a dime to upgrade to Pro, Gold, Silver or whatever your site of choice is calling it, you do not have the ability to send a man a message. It's a good idea to say that in your profile. Notice how I said - *But I can and I will add you to my hotlist if I think you're interesting.* It's a good idea to put something like that (or use that exact phrase) in your profile.

We'll get into the hotlist and how to use it later. You'll also notice I mentioned in my profile that I like starting dance floors. I put that in there not only because it's true, but also because it's a nice bonus if you can be fed and entertained! Just remember to meet the person at the dining establishment or the venue. There are no pick-ups at your house or apartment allowed and there is no meeting for just coffee or drinks, even if there is good music. You need sustenance and you can listen to the radio at home.

Upload a Picture

Dating for Food does not work without a picture, it just doesn't. You have to upload one. It does not matter if you are not a supermodel. You are adorable so long as you believe in yourself. Don't show your date that you think you're anything less than a great beauty. Be confident.

Confidence is very appealing to most men. In fact, share more than one picture so you come across as open and comfortable in your skin.

HERE ARE SOME PICTURE TIPS:

DO NOT post an outdated photo.

Don't post a photo from when you were fifteen and dreaming of being accepted at the Barbizon modeling school. As if. If you show up looking years older than your picture you can kiss an appetizer goodbye.

Post a Recent Adorable Picture of Yourself! You're cute!

DO NOT post a picture of your pet.

No one wants to see your kitty or your hound. They want to see you!

Plus, the guy is never going to come to your house if you are following the rules, so there is no need to share your pets (unless they happen to be with you in that adorable picture of you).

DO NOT post a picture of you with your kids. Do I really need to tell you this? Are you shopping for child molesters? No!

Well, guess what, child molesters are who just might hit you up if you post your kid's photos all over your profile. Leave your kids out of dating for food.

Don't put out bait for freaks and creeps.

DO NOT post an overly sexy picture.

You are dating for food, not a one-night hook-up. Sexy pictures will get you asked out for drinks, not dinner. You want dinner.

DO post a picture that looks like you. What is your best Facebook picture *that looks like you* that has gotten the most comments? Try that one. You're pretty.

DO smile! If you have a great smile, post a picture of you smiling. If you are missing teeth, don't. If you have fake teeth, for God's sake put them in for your photo.

DO post a picture of you having fun. Have any pictures of you laughing your ass off? Try some of those. You look awesome and happy. I'd take you out and feed you.

You can switch out pictures too in order to see which ones get you the most invites.

Chapter 5
BAITING YOUR HOOK

What You're Looking for
duh, food!

Here comes the fun part. This is the section where you fill out what you're looking for. Don't be a jerk and just put "food." Men have huge egos. Learn to rub them (the egos) and get fed.

DO NOT choose a specific age range, height

Do Not Discriminate When You're Hungry.

or hair color in your man/meal hunt. Select ages 18-80 because if an eighty-year-old man wants to take you to the buffet, you accept! If an eighteen-year-old saved up to take you to pizza, you go!

Here's what I wrote:

Meeting fellow rock stars, geeks, dorks, nerds and superheroes is always a pleasure. I love people. I love nerds. I love dorks and funny people and those who are smarter than me but don't rub my nose in it. I love philanthropists, artists, musicians and men who can build things. Those who are driven to do good things for the planet earn my respect and admiration. I have met people on this site that I ended up being good friends. I hope you're one of them! You never know what can happen. Meeting awesome men makes me as happy as a clam. Are clams happy? I'd love to figure that out. What do you think?

Notice how I put in that I like "geeks, dorks and nerds" right up front? That is because they are the coolest guys. If you haven't figured that out yet, take note. The super hunky guys usually want to meet for coffee and have you pick up the tab as they tell you about some script they are writing or want to star in.

I learned the *no coffee or drinks* rule after meeting a depressed documentary filmmaker out for coffee. Not only did I not even get a pastry, I sat there and wondered if the guy was going to kill himself right there in Starbucks. He was so depressed I wondered why he even bothered spending time with me. That guy needed a therapist, not a date.

Nerds are the Best Dates!

Nerds are my favorite choice for a date. Forget everything you thought about nerds in high school and give them a chance. They can usually afford to take you out because as nerds, they have good jobs because they're smart. They also have good taste compared to most of the super hunky guys. Male model types like to talk about their abs. I know because I fed and supported a few of them.

The studs can make you want to poke your eyes and eardrums out after a while. Nerds, on the other hand, are more likely to talk about things that interest you.

Don't discriminate against the overweight or unattractive either. Flush your prima donna standards down the toilet. The guys you would never be seen with might surprise you by being the most interesting people you've ever had the pleasure of dining with. Cease the judgments.

It's important to say that you're willing to date all sorts of men, but don't include negative comments like: "please don't be like my lying, cheating jerk ex." I experimented for a while in the "What I'm Looking For" section and I noticed that I got the most visits (and meals) when I kept it funny and supportive of men. You want to make it clear that you love men, even if you're still angry about the last boyfriend who stole your bank pin number.

CHAPTER 6

WARNING: SHARKS!

As you begin this process of online dating, (what I call "fishing for food"), you must remember you are entering the wild world of cyberspace. It can be a dangerous place. Everyone has access to it, and I mean *everyone*!

There are some real whack-job freaks out there and some of them will contact you! So you have to have a plan. You have to anticipate that a dangerous creep will try to date you and then you have to know exactly what step to take when you realize you might be in trouble.

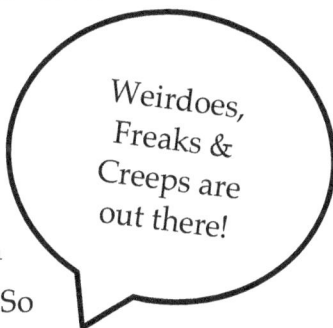

Weirdoes, Freaks & Creeps are out there!

I received emails from men who were simply gross. My advice is to hit the "delete" button and do not reply.

One guy sent me quite a few emails with pictures attached that showed him naked with an erect member! Ewww! DELETE!! (After you share it with all of your friends for a good laugh.)

In addition to the "delete" button, in the upper right corner there is an option to "Block User." Right under the options to Email Your Man, Poke Your Man, Wink at Your Man, See More Men Like Your Man, Forward Your Man to a Friend, and Get Your Man's Number there is a BLOCK option.

One of them is *Block from Contact*, which means you're blocking him from contacting you. *Block from Search* means he will no longer annoyingly show up when you search for meals (I mean men). Under those options there is a *Report This Profile* option. Use that if someone is really freaking you out or harassing you.

I never had to report anyone and I think that's pretty rare but you should know where the Report Abuse and the Block buttons are just in case! Most dating sites are set up in roughly the same format and will have a button that allows you to block unwanted users. Find this button on whatever site you use and do everything you can to Block All Sharks! You can also use the "Report Abuse" button if some shark is circling or biting at you.

BLOCK Sharks & Report Freaks!

Like I said, I had pretty good luck and was contacted by only two truly freaky guys including the one who sent me naked photos. The other one kept messaging me about a house he was staying at that had lots of rooms and he had lots of free time. It looked like a mass-email message that he sent to every female online. Don't respond to anything that seems like a mass-mailing.

Trust your instincts. Your gut is a great sensor. And by all means if you get a message from a guy in a sweater in Santa Monica with the subject line, "Looking for someone to play with" – use the Block feature quickly!

If you do your best screening and you still end up on a date with a weirdo, you need to have a plan. We will cover this again in Chapter 17 – *Weirdoes, Freaks and Creeps* but for now, make a note to watch out for the sharks because even though the attacks are very few, you have to learn to fearlessly use the power you have in the Delete and Block buttons to prevent as many creeps as possible from landing on your hook when you go fishing for food!

CHAPTER 7

IGNORE BOBBERS, YOU WANT BITES

You need to know that on your dating profile, there will be some men who want only to message you. It's odd, I know. I have no idea why some guys only want to send messages, and never actually get

Don't Spend Too Much Time Messaging.

together in person, but some men just get off on the thrill of electronic communications. Maybe they are lonely and very, very shy, and they just want an Internet Buddy. Maybe they are not who they say they are. Maybe it's really an old lady pretending to be a man. You can never know for sure because it's the Internet where anonymity is easy.

There's one simple rule about these types of "message only buddies".

Do NOT waste your time sending messages back and forth. You need to focus on the messages from guys who will feed you food!

You Must Meet In Person – For a Meal!

One guy who messaged me seemed OK at first, but then he started sending me long drawn out novellas about his life, his future, his dreams etc. It took so much time to read his stuff, I simply stopped opening his messages. Don't get me wrong, it's good to get to know people, and reading someone's life story can be very revealing. But not every drawn-out message is a worthy read.

Plus, if you're going to listen to a life story, you might as well be eating! Avoid wasting your time online. Seriously.

There are far too many weirdoes in their basements that you will never meet, thankfully, but who will try to be your online pen pal. They will message you endless stories so long as you listen. Then, get this - they get angry if you stop paying attention. Strange, I know, but it is both awful and humorous at the same time. The guy who sent long life stories to me started saying he was furious with me when I didn't respond to the details of his messages. Note that I never met the guy and only responded to him once with a note that read: *Hey, thanks for the message! I'd love to get together. I am supper busy this week but I can fit in a meal.* (Notice the intentional misspelling of super as supper – subliminal messages!)

He was apparently upset that I did not answer his diatribes with the same number of words!

After he started sending messages that made it sound as though we were a committed couple who had a lovers' spat, I deleted everything from the guy and blocked him from communicating with me again. Freak.

I mention this crazy guy because people like him will probably message you, too. And while you can't stop them from finding you, initially, if you're online dating, you can put the brakes on quickly and keep them out of your online space.

The best way to avoid creeps is to not answer them in first place, but it's hard to know that someone is a creep until you communicate a little bit and read what they write and get a sense of what kind of person they are from what they say and how they say it. So you might have to let the guy on your hook for a bit - as long as you're willing to cut the line fast.

Sticking with the fishing metaphor for a moment, we'll get more into throw back on Chapter 17 – *Weirdoes, Freaks and Creeps.*

Keep Reading.

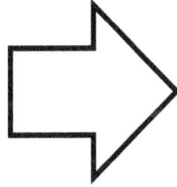

DELETE WEIRDOES WHO DON'T FEED YOU

If you message back and forth for too long with a guy who does not come out and ask you to breakfast, lunch, dinner or a late-night meal – give it up. You are done. If you continue any longer with this guy, you'll starve to death. A girl's got to eat. You are not looking for some sob story who can't pull himself away from the computer. You are looking for food.

Bottom line - avoid the bobbers out there who will just nibble at your profile and message you without giving you nutrition. If he's not a feeder, throw him back and keep fishing.

CHAPTER 8
FISHING FOR FEEDERS

CAST INTO THE ONLINE SEA

Now that you've set up your profile and put it out there for the whole world to see that you're looking for a nourishing date (without coming right out and saying "a free meal"), you have to be strategic. Think about it as if you're going fishing. Whether you're fishing for small mouth bass or big mouth men, it's all in the technique.

Look at all the Men(u) Items!.

Or in shopping terms, imagine scrolling through the racks of humans and selecting the ones you'd like to take to the dressing room.

If you took that to mean anything sexual, skip ahead and read Chapter 10 – *Check Yourself – Not Him.*

I'm not saying you should take your date for a hook-up at the local Macy's Department store! I'm talking about scrolling through the many profiles of men like you're moving through the racks of dresses at your favorite shop or better yet, your favorite aisle at the grocery store. It's like you're pushing your cart down the aisle of men, picking out profiles you like. You don't purchase them; you just select which ones to put into your cart. Your cart in online dating is your "Hot List."

Put Men Into Your "Hot List"

Right next to the profile there is an option to "Add to Hot List." On some sites it is called "Add to Favorites."

Your site of choice can call it whatever they like but to us who are Dating for Food is our grocery cart! When you see a guy that you'd like to sit across from for dinner, add him to your **Hot List!**

Don't forget, just because you put something in your cart while grocery shopping doesn't mean you have to buy it. You can always change your mind when you get to the register. It's the same when you're *Dating for Food.* Put a few men in your Hot List and see what happens. You can always choose to remove them later.

Men Love Being put on Your Hotlist!

There's nothing that strokes a man's ego better than putting him into a hot list. Of course, the guy won't know you put him on your "hotlist" because you're thinking (or should be) about a hot meal rather than hot sex, but so what.

The guys you "hotlist" will receive a notice on their own profile that you "hot listed" them. Men like that. Trust me. All men want to be thought of as hot and they will check out any woman who sees them that way. They can't help themselves. They will check you out.

You will get these kinds of notices too. There's a place for "who's viewing you" and "who's put you into a hot list." It's very valuable information because it helps you shop more efficiently for the guys who will feed you the nourishing food you need. Pay attention to who thinks you're hot. If you see that someone has listed you on their HotList, list them back! That's a way to tug at your line a bit.

Be aware that the guys you put in your "Hot List" will look at your picture and your headline and usually skim your profile. That's why you want to be sure your profile is interesting, charming and fun.

Men do not like crazy evil cranky women although they sometimes marry them, usually because of mommy issues. But usually, if they are halfway sane, they don't want to spend an evening with a mean high maintenance witch.

Most men who are dating online want to have some fun. And yes, it's true that most of them want to move from the dinner table to the bedroom, but you're not going to let that happen. Your plan is to eat a good meal and go home, alone. You'll be too bloated for sex anyway. Plus, you'll have gas from the huge meal you just stuffed yourself with.

Sex should not be on your brain in the first place. That can wait until you have your life in order. We're getting to that party. We'll talk more about possible digestion problems, like whether to eat garlic or not, in Chapter 13 – *What to Order & How to Save It.*

Remember, you are putting men in your "Hot List," you are not messaging them! Why, you ask? Because you signed up for a standard free account and you do not have the ability to send messages unless you upgrade. You can only send messages if you upgrade to gold or silver, but don't do it! Do not spend one time to message any man. Do you hear me? If you feel tempted, go reread Chapter 2 – *The Rules!*

This means you have to depend on men (or fishes) to bite at your bait (or profile). The most important step in getting a man to message you is putting him in your "Hot List." It's very simple.

CHAPTER 9

BAITING YOUR FISH

TUG THE LINE – MESSAGE HIM

You've got a fish on-line! A man is biting at your profile. You have to know when to snap your wrist, when to let out a little line and when to sit absolutely still. It's like the deer creeping over into the hunter's campsite. You can't make a lot of noise or you scare the deer away. If the guy shows a little interest - the cyber

Wink Back at the Men(u)!

equivalent of, let's say, winking at you form the other end of the bar, what do you do? Easy. You wink back!

You are a good girl and have followed the rules and haven't spent any money on a dating.

You might be unable to wink unless he winks at you first. Perfect. Wink back. You shouldn't wink first anyway. You already know that the only thing you're allowed to do in the beginning is put men in your "Hot List."

When you get a response, assess the nature of the contact and respond in kind - nothing more - nothing less. If you get more than a wink, you can respond more aggressively, but don't ever overdo it. If he keeps winking and never sends an actual message, go back and read Chapter 7 if necessary to remind yourself to – *Ignore Bobbers, You Want Bites.*

When you get a full on message from a guy, congratulations! Even though you're only looking for food, it's a good ego boost to be hit on sometimes.

Getting a message means you can almost hear the dinner bell chiming. Those are Dinner Bells not Wedding Bells!

Remember ladies; getting a message from a man you're hoping to date for food is not a love letter. There's no fat little Cupid knocking on your door. It's the delivery boy, and he knows you're hungry. Answer the door and be nice.

You "answer the door" by clicking on the message link. You need to check your messages as quickly as possible. There is no need to follow those other *Rules* and keep a guy waiting for three days when you're hungry. Read the message and see if he'd be a good dinner date (or lunch or breakfast). If it's the guy from Santa Monica in the sweater, delete it without delay. If he seems halfway decent, which will be true about most of the guys who message you, answer him back!

Don't be shy and by all means, remember what I said in Chapter 5 - Do not discriminate on the guy's age or looks.

You do not have to put the poor guy through hell and drive him mad trying to get in touch with you. You are available – for breakfast, lunch and dinner!

HERE ARE A FEW EXAMPLE RESPONSES:

(I've tried them all myself. They really work. Use them yourself, and let me know what happens.)

Hey, thank you for the message. Love your profile! I'm super busy this week, but I'd love to meet you in town. Let me know if lunch or dinner works. Hope you're having a great day!

Thanks for the message. What a great profile you have. I look forward to meeting you in person and sharing a meal. My days are pretty full working, but I can meet for dinner.

Thanks for the message. You are so funny! I can't wait to share a meal and hear more about what you're up to. Let's do something spontaneous. Brazilian food? Yum!

You get the picture. Be short, cute and busy, but available to eat. Go write out some replies to be ready. I'll wait for you. Don't worry; I'll be eating during the break.

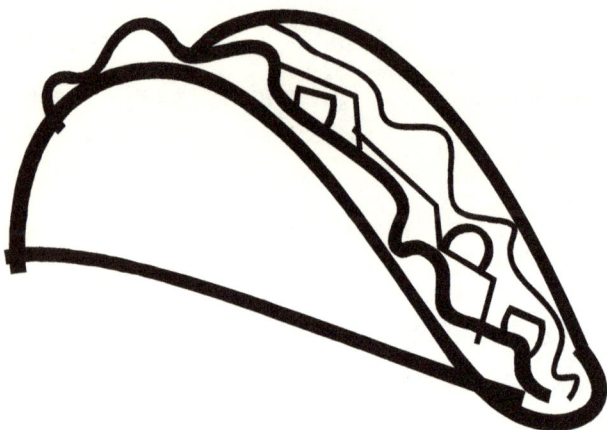

CHAPTER 10
CHECK YOURSELF OUT, NOT HIM

You're going on a date!

If you have followed the rules, you are meeting at the

> Don't Just Meet for Drinks. Duh.

eating establishment. You are not meeting for drinks or coffee. Gas is too expensive to go out just for drinks. This is *Will Date 4 Food*, not *Will Date for Libations*. It doesn't matter if it's breakfast, lunch, dinner or a late-night snack – if you're putting the time into getting all fancied up and driving someplace to meet a guy, you at least need to replace the energy your body used up to get you there!

A martini or a glass of wine is fine, so long as you pair with real nutrition (bar snacks don't count - neither do French fries)! You're trying to feed your whole body, not just pack slabs of fat on your thighs.

Speaking about your lovely body, remember to dress well. You want to show up looking as cute as can be but please leave the pigtails at home. There's a difference between being cute and a lunatic. I only say this because I've done it myself. This is no time to show off your fuzzy pompom hair clips and your neon pink lipstick that matches your neon pink clogs. Do not dress slutty either. You do not need to reveal your loads of cleavage or your pronounced nipples by not wearing a bra. Both are equally distracting. Leave the skirt with the slit up to your ass home too. You're not a slut going alone to sit at a bar and pick up someone up after they've already eaten. Be classy and cute.

Guys want to FEED dates that are classy and self-respecting. They want to do another F-word to the dates who show up half naked. Think job interview at Google.

Don't wear too much make-up, but wear some. Your date (if you follow the rules) will never see what you look like first thing in the morning so no need to show up looking like you just got out of bed. Cover your dark circles from lack of nutrition with cover up, but don't make yourself look too radiant. You don't want to make him uncomfortable and nervous around such a Goddess as yourself. Be the girl he wants to chat with while he watches you eat. You're so cute when you're chewing.

If you're like me and had a bad habit of shopping at the highbrow department stores like Barneys, get over yourself.

Get to Know Your Dime Store!

You can find what you need at your local dime store or drugstore. Then use just enough cover up to get rid of the really noticeable stuff like dark circles and big pimples.

Don't use so much make-up that it gets all caked in lines on your face. You don't want the guy to know you used cover-up - Duh. Try the mineral cover-up first because it is much less noticeable than the creamy gunk. Then add a dash of color to your lips and rose up your cheeks a tiny bit. I use my lipstick for lip and cheek color because, you guessed it - it's cheaper! Forget about lip liner and gobs of lipstick. Why, you ask? Because YOU'RE EATING! Too much lipstick is especially disgusting because it gets all over the place when you eat and it looks gross on the bread and your fork, and smeared all over your glass. Be classy, not trashy.

Comb your hair.

If you have crazy curly hair like I do and combing it will make you look like you escaped from an insane asylum, don't comb it. Tame it. Pin it up. You'll look pretty.

Make sure your teeth are clean. I'm serious. Double check. Clean your ears too. Check your breath. Floss and scrape your tongue. Not that you'll be kissing anyone, but nasty breath is just that – nasty.

Make sure your nails are presentable too. A hand with dirty nails picking up a wine class is not attractive. In fact, it can ruin a guy's appetite and the next thing you know you're headed home hungry because you didn't make it past appetizers.

I made the mistake once of rushing out to a date after digging in the garden. What was I thinking? When I saw my nails had a layer of dirt under them, I quickly started asking my date questions while I cleaned my nails under the table.

I was horrified but thankfully I noticed it before I picked up my glass. I kept my hands neatly folded in my lap, with my napkin, and cleaned my nails as I LISTENED to my date talk about his work schedule. (We're getting into the art of Listening coming up!)

Remember what we talked about in Chapter 4? You do not have to be a supermodel to successfully Date 4 Food. (Although most models could really use *a good meal!*) You are awesome. You are pretty and you deserve a good meal.

CHAPTER 11

GET TO KNOW YOUR DATE

THAT MEANS LISTEN

Yes, get to know your date! Can you imagine that? Even if you're certain he will never be the one you take home to Mama, get to know him. He is a fellow human being who is willing to feed you. Bless his heart. Listen to him. If you're eating, you are not talking anyway. Why not listen for crying out loud?

LISTEN! You Might Learn Something!

Believe me, the more you listen, the more you will be fed. Keep him talking. If he's the least bit normal, he will love to talk about himself.

It's not just a guy thing, most people like to talk about themselves and most people have interesting stories to tell. In between bites (and after you swallow) ask more questions to keep him talking and really listen to what he is saying. Enjoy his company for exactly who he is, not as someone you want him to be.

Here's the catch (we will go further into this in Chapter 20 – *The Best Catch Ever*), when you listen, you get to know and love your fellow man! And I'm not talking about you falling in love with the guy you could never picture yourself with in a million years. I'm talking about loving your fellow man as another awesome human on this Earth. But how can you know if he's awesome if you don't listen to him? And how can you listen if you're busy talking about yourself and your truckload of issues? We'll get more into your issues in the next chapter – *Check Your Issues with the Valet.*

It is easier to listen to someone when you are not talking. If he's not talking – ask him questions about himself. Then eat while he answers. Duh.

QUESTIONS TO ASK

How do you like what you're doing?

Seen any good movies lately?

What are you reading?

How's your family?

What's the worst date you ever went on?

What's the grossest thing you've ever seen?

What do you love about this city?

What pisses you off the most?

Do you like where you live?

What do you believe in?

Had any strange experiences?

What would you change about the world?

Is there anything you regret?

If you could learn anything new, what would it be?

What's your favorite food?

What's the best place you've ever eaten at?

Do you have a favorite restaurant?

Why is it your favorite?

What's your favorite drink?

Would you want psychic abilities if you could have them?

What's your favorite thing to do?

Ever committed a crime?

How do you keep your life in order?

Are you a good accountant? Do you have one?

Who do you most admire?

How do you feel about debt, the national kind?

What was your favorite cartoon as a kid?

Notice NONE of those questions had to do with love, politics, religion, his ring size, what his inseam was or where he wants to honeymoon! Ask questions that have nothing to do with stressful or romantic things, and everything to do with him, fun stuff and food.

WHAT IF HE GETS ALL **ROMANTIC?**

Well, do you like the guy? But wait, this is not about romance! You are not looking for a boyfriend. But things do happen and real feelings can come up when you're enjoying a free meal.

If you do end up meeting a romantic interest while Dating for Food, it's best to tell him what you're up to. You need to see if he's okay with you going out for food dates, and if not is he willing and able to keep you fed? It would be a little strange to be going out with other men for food when you have a boyfriend. It's disrespectful, I think. But I tend to be polite.

If you're a total jerk, I guess you could be married and still out dating for food. Who knows, maybe your husband can become the master chef of Recipes from Leftovers! But **Will Date 4 Food** is not about being a jerk. It's about eating while listening to your fellow man (you may learn something).

If you're not interested and your date starts to get all mushy on you, let him down gently or distract him. Bring the conversation back to the food. If you say point blank that you're not interested in him, you're food source could be gone!

Talk about what you're eating. Talk about what he's eating. Ask him what his favorite food is. If he starts talking about wedding cake, you're in trouble. Skip ahead to Chapter 17 – *Weirdoes, Freaks and Creeps*.

While we're on the subject romance, let me tell you a little story:

When I was dating for food I received a message from a guy without a picture. For the most part, I never responded to profiles without pictures. But this guy attached a picture to his message and it turned out I knew him. We had been at dinner parties together in Hollywood and he was pretty famous. Okay, he was a soap star. Yes, he was online dating. For him to go out to a dark bar where no one could see him was simply out of the question. He was actually the most vain person I've ever met in my life. He would get into a mood if less than four people recognized him in a day. Shoot me. Anyway, he hit me up for dinner and we went out.

Okay, we got totally hot and heavy. What can I say? Vain or not, he was pretty hot. He was the first and only date I ever came clean with. I fessed up that I was working on a project called **Will Date 4 Food.** He thought it was hilarious but he did not want me to go on dates, even if I was working on a How-To book.

Here's the dilemma, Ladies. I liked this guy. I told him that I was not actually "dating" but duh, I still needed to eat. I didn't come up with this idea just to be funny. I really had gone broke supporting starving artists. I wasn't lying. I know you can understand. You've been there. So when Soap Star wanted me to quit dating other men, even if it was for food, I asked him if he planned on feeding me. He laughed. He thought I was so funny, which I am. But I was serious.

That's when he said that of course, he would feed me. And he did, for a while.

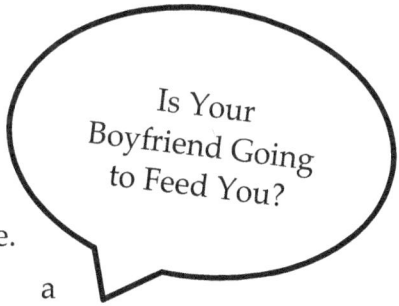

Is Your Boyfriend Going to Feed You?

But he didn't realize that I was actually hungry – really hungry. Okay, so I snuck in a few breakfast and lunch dates for food while he was shooting his shows. I had to. I was hungry.

You want me to starve?

Then I got a book deal. It was a pretty good one too and the exact amount I needed to get out of debt. God Bless America. So on one of our romantic dates I mentioned to Soap Star how I giddy I was now that I had a book deal and would soon be out of debt. I added that it was wonderful how he didn't cost me any money and how starving artists were in my past!

Soap Star just stared at me, speechless. He asked if I really had debt and I said, nonchalantly, "Well, yeah, doesn't everyone? This is America."

That night when I got home, I received a text message from him that said, simply. "We're breaking up." Apparently having debt is like having the plague. When I reminded him, laughing, that we had met because I was online dating for food, he did not LOL back.

I hadn't started this project to look for a boyfriend anyway, so I went back in search for food. I won't lie though. I felt gross and dumb.

Why was I in debt in the first place? Why had I been so stupid to pay for everyone else in the first place? Why hadn't I cared for myself better?

Actually, the answer is right there in the dedication of this book: Why don't you turn back and reread it?

In fact, here it is:

Dedicated to all the hungry girls and women who have gone into debt supporting starving artist boyfriends, deadbeat husbands, miscellaneous family members, and who still insist on picking up the check or going Dutch. Ladies, it is time for you to eat.

I dedicated this book to you so that you don't suffer the way I did. It's not that a little debt is shameful, but I don't want you to dig yourself into a hole trying to make everyone else happy when you're own health is suffering because you're starving to death and you need to take care of yourself.

Let me remind you that you're dating for food because you need to eat, not because you want another boyfriend. It's nice to have dinner with an interesting guy without worrying about the baggage that comes with serious boyfriends like Soap Man with his own truckload of issues.

While Dating for Food, it's best to stop thinking about romance and trying to find Mr. Perfect. Get your life in order and focus on your hungry belly instead of the chiseled face of some Soap Star.

And by all means - try to get out and stay out of debt. We'll get to that in Chapter 16 – *When You're Not Dating* but in the meantime…

FORGET ROMANCE.

FOCUS ON THE FOOD.

CHAPTER 12

CHECK YOUR ISSUES
WITH THE VALET

DON'T BE CRAZY

There is no reason whatsoever to go blabbing to your date that you've read this book and that you're dating for food. If you do that, you can kiss dessert goodbye. Keep your mouth chewing.

In fact, you should not talk

Your Date is NOT Your Therapist.

much about yourself at all. You know what your problems are; share them on Facebook, not with your date. Get a therapist. Oh right, you probably can't afford one. Call your mother! If your mother is nuts, call your gay best friend. If you do not have a gay buddy go reread Chapter 3 – *Your Dating Buddy aka The Gay Mafia.*

But whatever you do, DO NOT talk to your date about your problems! It's not that your problems aren't important. But you have to think strategically about how to date4food. Your life and your finances are obviously not in good shape or you would not be reading this book. You got yourself into this mess because you're a co-dependent woman who tries to take care of everyone but yourself. It's all on your shoulders, isn't it? I know. I had the same problem. That's why I am urging you to check your issues at the door, or with the valet. (Actually you should not be paying for valet. The tip alone could buy you the next day's lunch. Park down the block and walk or be dropped off and picked up by your gay watchdog). Just leave your woes someplace else before you sit down for dinner and zip your lip even if the guy asks you outright about your troubles. Tell him life is wonderful and ask him a question before you take a bite!

Going on a *Date 4 Food* is not a time to share your issues. You are not going to tell some guy about your financial woes (unless of course he's an accountant, but then he will probably charge you).

Not only are you going to keep quiet about your finances, you are going to keep your mouth shut about your romantic past, present and future. You are not on a date for romance. You are there for the food. Drill that into your brain (but not in the psycho Jeffrey Dahmer way – just make sure you stick to the rule). Whenever you forget that you're dating for food, go back to Chapter 2 and reread *The Rules!* Rip them out and keep them in your wallet. Or go to **WillDate4Food.com** and print them out.

But I know what you are going to do because most women think the same exact way about their dates. No matter whom we go out with, we look at the guy as a potential mate. We can't help it.

From the first moment we see his profile picture, we're wondering what our mother will think of him. We wonder whether he's a good kisser, whether he's got a good financial (and other) package and whether he could be, might be, the one!

You must trust me on this and listen very

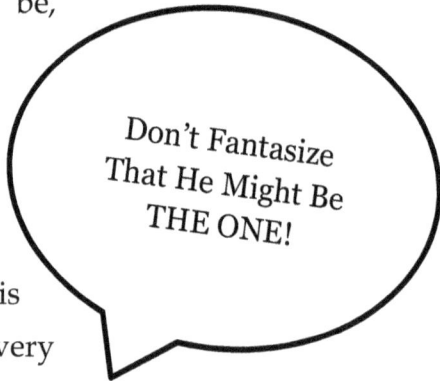

Don't Fantasize That He Might Be THE ONE!

carefully to what I'm about to say: Tell your little brain to "shut the hell up". Erase those fantasies from your mind immediately. Push whatever STOP button you can find. Slap yourself in the face if you have to (actually, don't do that). I know it's hard but you must not project your fantasies on your food dates! I see you shaking your head. You think it's impossible but it isn't.

Your fantasy is not important right now and it will make your date very uncomfortable. Plus, it's a fantasy!

Do not project any of your daydreaming nonsense onto your date. Check yourself and your issues before you even step foot into the eating establishment. Do I need to remind you that you also felt like that mooch ex was "the one" when you first met him too? You're nodding. That's because you fell into the trap of projecting what you wanted onto someone who kinda sorta fit the profile. Stop daydreaming about finding "the one." In fact, stop daydreaming period.

Dating for Food is serious business. Not only do you need to focus on being fed and listening to men you normally would not have given a second glance to, but you are going to get your life together. It's coming up in Chapter 16.

Stopping the projection is a particularly important requirement for those of you who have a past history where violence was perpetrated against you by the male species. If you tend to think all men are despicable, you need to leave those issues at the door when you're dating for food.

Dating for Food is not the time to project your evil uncle onto your innocent date. Your date is not every single guy who ever broke your heart. He is not your therapist. This is good practice for you not to project your issues onto all men.

When you're dating4food, you cannot, under any circumstances, berate, belittle or badmouth men. You should not be talking anyway. You should be eating. If your date has a strange or irritating answer to anything, shake it off. Have a drink. Smile. Focus on finishing your plate (More on what to order in the next chapter).

Last but not least, do *not* get into a debate with your date. I don't care if you were the debating queen in high school, don't pick a fight - and don't indulge him if he tries to pick one with you. For example, if he tells you he voted for someone who makes you want to move out of the country, don't pass out at the table. Ask him questions about the candidate and why he likes them, but don't offer up your own opinions. Learn about his instead.

Who cares whom he voted for anyway? You're not there to run a campaign; you are there to eat. If he continues to talk politics, ask him to vote for his favorite menu item. Use the voting theme in the conversation to direct him toward a less contentious topic, like what you're thinking of ordering for dessert.

CHAPTER 13
WHAT TO ORDER
& HOW TO SAVE IT

THINK LEFTOVERS!

I know you're hungry, but do not be a witch and order the most expensive thing on the menu. Think about the future. Think about what you can order that you can also take home and eat for breakfast and lunch the next day. Lobster makes for skanky leftovers, it really does. Plus, your date might never pay for a second meal if he thinks you're trying to bankrupt his entertainment budget.

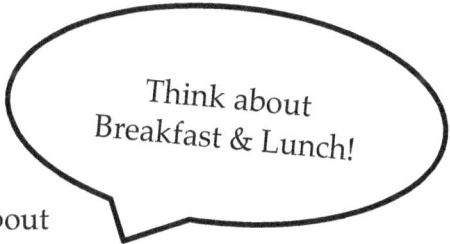

Think about Breakfast & Lunch!

Order like you have to feed a houseful of starving kids at home – go for the family value items like pasta and potpies. Family style options tend to be cheaper anyway, especially pasta, and they heat up really well the next day. Think about feeding the starving kids at home - and that starving kid is YOU!

Think of yourself as your own baby. Seriously. Treat yourself with the same kindness you would use to take care of a real baby. (If you really do have starving kids at home there are plenty of organizations out there that will help get you and your kids fed for free. If you need a job in addition to a good meal, you might consider mentioning this to your date, but remember, don't make it too depressing! Skip ahead to Chapter 16 for more advice on these serious issues – *When You're Not Dating*).

Back to your menu options.

No matter how much you want the filet and lobster, you run the risk of not being asked out again if you order it. But if you order something reasonably priced, and you keep your date talking by asking questions and listening to him, you probably will be asked out again.

This isn't complicated. If you're a decent, reasonable gal, you'll win lots of repeat dates with feeders! But if you are a witch, a jerk, a pig or a cow, you probably will not be asked out again. Mind your manners and order well.

If you are a vegetarian or a vegan, dating for food will be harder on you than others but fortunately there is usually something for you at pretty much every food establishment. Except maybe the BBQ places. You'll probably be stuck with coleslaw and beans if you agree to eat BBQ, but the upside is – it will make you nice and gassy which will kill any urge you might have to go home with the guy for a hook-up.

GARLIC OR NO GARLIC?

There's no way you are going to be making out with your date or snuggling up in the back of his pick-up, so there's no reason to avoid garlic.

Don't be a Slut. Eat Garlic.

In fact, it could be a perfect deterrent if your date turns out to be a weirdo (or a vampire)! Even if you start feeling frisky, your date won't be interested anyway if you reek. Plus, eating a lot of garlic will protect you from breaking the rules if you tend to slide down that slippery slut path.

BEHAVE YOURSELF

Use your manners. Don't talk with your mouth full. It's not pretty. Don't slouch. That's not pretty either.

Confident women sit up tall and proud. Do not text. Do not look at your phone. Put it on silent and keep it in your bag or your pocket. That is silent, not vibrate. The last thing you want is for your phone to start vibrating right when your date is the middle of telling a very long detailed story about himself. Not only will you interrupt him, you might make him lose his focus and start asking you questions!

I know you're there to eat, but don't stuff your face. We're in a recession, not a full blow depression (yet). You don't have to go shoveling food into your mouth like you might not eat again for weeks. You are dining out, not pigging out.

Do not get drunk. It's not attractive. Set yourself to a two drink maximum if you're a drinker. If he orders a bottle of wine, have two glasses from the bottle, tops. If you get too tipsy or God forbid inebriated, your dating for food Rules can go out the window, especially if he's a sexy geek.

You may wake up and find yourself having breakfast with the guy! And I don't mean meeting him at the restaurant either, I mean rolling over and seeing him in the AM. Not good. If you've already forgotten about why this is a bad thing to do, please go back and re-read Chapter 2 – *The Rules!* Print them out for God's sake and take them with you on EVERY date.

If you're thinking about drinking alcohol, excuse yourself, go to the bathroom and read the Rules BEFORE you get drunk because your vision won't work well if you wait until the third drink to remind yourself of why that third drink was a very bad idea.

Save Your Leftovers

If you order correctly, you will have enough to take home. Don't worry. It's not rude. Everyone does it, or they should!

If your date asks why you want take-out,

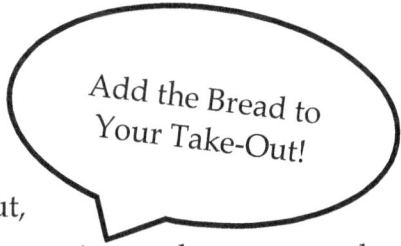

Add the Bread to Your Take-Out!

tell him you have a dog or that your mother is staying with you and she likes snacks. Then he won't get any ideas about trying to come over for a late night snack.

Make sure to save the bread! You might think it's totally useless since it will just get old and hard, but there is where you are wrong. Hard bread is perfect for bread soup!

You'll be amazed what you can do with leftovers. Most leftovers are great if you just heat them up and put a fried egg on top of it for breakfast. But we'll get more into detail about recipes next. Remember, lobster and most fishy dishes don't keep well and they smell funny. Think about your leftovers when you're ordering! You're not just eating one meal when you're on a date, you're preparing for a delicious future, too.

CHAPTER 14

WILL DATE 4 FOOD RECIPES

BONUS – FREE RECIPES

On the days when you do not have dates, you will not treat yourself by taking yourself out. You will not spend any more money. You will cook at home and use your leftovers from your dates. Duh.

This re-gifting of your Dating 4 Food leftovers - to yourself - is

Use Your Leftovers & Cook at Home!

going to help you become self-sufficient and a good cook at the same time! You can skip this chapter and go on to Chapter 15 – *Getting Action (not that kind)* if you're not in the cooking mood because we're about to get into some yummy stuff.

LAST NIGHT'S LEFTOVERS
FRITTATA

Not only is **Dating for Food** good for your finances, it will allow you to practice your culinary skills as well. Most leftovers from decent restaurants can be made into a frittata. If you don't know what a frittata is, Google it. It's a glorified baked omelet. Yum. Imagine yourself putting all your favorite ingredients into an omelet, then imagine covering it with cheese and putting the whole omelet into an oven so it comes out like a casserole. That's a frittata.

If you're having friends over (like your other girlfriends who are Dating 4 Food or your gay best friend), frittatas are perfect because you can hide things in a frittata. For example, my personal favorite leftover for a frittata is a burrito (especially if it has guacamole and sour cream in it).

You can't just reheat an old burrito and make it look good, but you can mash it up and put it into a frittata! That way no one will ever know they're eating your leftovers from a date night, unless they're in on it, in which case, they should try to fool you with a frittata too. Create a guessing game about where the leftovers are from. The whole point of these recipes is to make sure we are stretching the food into future meals that are not only clever ways to reuse food but are scrumptious!

You don't want to use anything in a frittata with

Don't Put Bones in Your Frittata!

bones in it. Don't use the leftover fish or chicken with bones. You might choke and die. That would be bad. Think about food that would work well in a medley - like rice, beans, burritos, pot roast (yes, it works), potatoes, veggies, meatloaf, chicken potpie, and steak. Pasta doesn't work too well with this recipe either. It's mushy.

WHAT YOU NEED:

- A pan that you can put into the oven. (Cast iron is the best. If you don't have a cast iron pot, shame on you, use any small frying pan that does not have a rubber handle so you can put it into the oven.

- Olive Oil or butter to grease your pan

- 3 cloves of chopped garlic (if you like that sort of thing)

- 1 chopped Onion (if you like that sort of thing)

- Spinach, Broccoli, or Veggie of choice. (If you like that sort of thing)

- **Your leftovers from last night**

- 6-8 eggs

- Cheese of your choice. Cheddar works. I like Monterey Jack with jalapenos.

- Salt and Pepper to taste

- Parmesan or Romano cheese for the top

What You Do:

1. Heat up your skillet on the stovetop to medium-high heat. While your pan is heating chop or mash up your last night's dinner depending on what it is. Once your pan is hot, put in your butter or olive oil and fry up your onions or garlic if you like that sort of thing. If you don't, skip that step. I personally like butter. Did I mention that I am a Southern gal?

2. Preheat your oven to 375. Crack your eggs into a bowl. You may just get some shells in there and it's easier to pick them out in a bowl instead of the pan. Beat the eggs until blended. Then pour your eggs into the hot pan. Let it cook for a minute. Then put in your leftovers. Mash it in there with your spatula. Top with veggie of your choice, spinach works well.

Skip this part if you hate veggies. Dash in salt and pepper.

You can put cayenne pepper in there too if you're a hottie like me. Top with slices of cheese. Sprinkle with the Parmesan or Romano.

3. Take the whole skillet and put it into the oven. Use an oven mitt for crying out loud. Don't hurt yourself. Bake at 375 for about 35-45 minutes. Take it out of the oven, let it cool on your stovetop, slice it and eat it.

While enjoying the spectacular flavors, pat yourself on the head and rejoice along with me: "God Bless **Will Date 4 Food.**" Aren't you happy that you're eating and you're learning to cook?

OODLES OF NOODLES

Like burritos, you can also make pretty much anything with pasta. Just use your noodle (haha). If you care about good flavors, do not use the same old tomato sauce in a can when you cook up your Date4Food leftover pasta. Try this instead:

WHAT YOU NEED:

- Olive oil to heat up your pan
- Pasta of your choice
- Squash and/or Zucchini (they are cheap)
- A package of Goat Cheese
- 3-5 chopped garlic cloves
- 1 chopped onion
- Your leftovers from last night. Sausage is the best but you can use whatever you have. You can use veggies too.
- Salt and Pepper for taste.

What You Do:

1. Get your water boiling in your pasta pot at the same time you heat up your skillet. It's called multi-tasking. Once your skillet is hot, pour in a dash of Olive Oil, and then your garlic and onion. Cook them until the onions are clear and the garlic is just a tad colored. Don't burn it for crying out loud. Then put in your sliced or chopped squash and zucchini with your leftovers. Stir it all while your water boils.

2. In the time it takes your water to boil and your pasta to cook, your concoction is ready. After you drain your pasta, put it back into the pot with your goat cheese. Stir the goat cheese around until the pasta is nice and coated. Add your leftover mixture. Dash in some salt and pepper. Eat it.

CO-DEPENDENT CASSEROLE

Casseroles are good and incredibly versatile too! You should add them to your recipe repertoire.

WHAT YOU NEED:

- Your leftovers (de-boned chicken, turkey, veggies, meat or duck.
- 2-3 cups of leftover pasta or rice (or you can make it if you have it. Rice is super cheap)
- 3-5 chopped cloves of garlic
- 1 chopped onion
- 3 long green onions, thinly sliced or chives
- 1 sliced leek (leeks are good, use them)
- 1 cup milk
- 1 cup grated cheese of your choice
- 1 cup cheese topping like Parmesan or Gruyere.

- 2 Tablespoons of Butter (or half a short stick if you're a butter nut like me)
- Half a cup of flour or cornstarch
- Salt and Pepper to taste
- Cayenne pepper or hot flakes (if you like that sort of thing)
- Butter or Pam

Yeah, I know that's a lot of ingredients but you should have the staples on hand anyway. Plus, it's still cheaper than eating out and you will have enough to be able to eat this for a few days. Quit complaining.

WHAT YOU DO:

1. Grease that pan with some butter or some spray on Pam if you have it. You'll think you just went back in time. Dump your leftovers along with your pasta or rice into a baking dish. A nice rectangle one is good.

If you don't have that size, use two smaller ones. Make it work. Line the bottom with your goods, including the leeks and green onions.

2. Melt your butter into a medium pan. Over medium heat, sauté the garlic and onion until the desired texture, usually when the onions are clear and the garlic is barely browning. Lower the heat and stir in your flour or cornstarch until you make a mess. It will be like a paste. Add the milk and stir until it is thick, slowing adding your cheese of choice.

3. As you're stirring preheat your oven to 350 degrees. Season your milk mixture to taste. I like tons of pepper, garlic salt and cayenne pepper myself. Pour that goo all over your leftovers waiting in the pan. Line the top with Gruyere or sprinkle Parmesan. Bake it for about 40 min.

You can do whatever you like with this recipe by using different types of cheeses, pasta instead of rice and the insides of your turkey sandwich verses that pot roast.

NICE PRICE RICE
(or quinoa but nothing rhymes with that)

Whatever else is in your kitchen, rice is a must-have item. It goes well with almost all types of leftovers and it's cheap! You can also use quinoa, which is healthier than rice and good if you have issues with wheat and some grains that cause you to have gas. Plus, guinoa is a complete protein. Bonus! But you should have rice on hand too. Not only is rice way cheaper but you can buy a gigantic bag at a discount store like Costco. (But don't EVER pay for a membership. Find a few friends who have memberships and go with them, duh. I bet your gay best friend has a membership.)

WHAT YOU NEED:

- Rice (or quinoa)
- Your leftovers
- Olive Oil

What You Do

1. Follow the directions on the package of rice or quinoa.
2. Put the cooked grains in a pan with a little bit of veggie oil or olive oil and fire it up with your leftovers. Stir it up. You're making fried rice! Look at you go.

Fried rice works with the frittata too, so you can double utilize your leftovers by having frittata with a burrito one day and frittata with rice the next!

BREAD SOUP

Ah, the gem of them all – bread soup. Bread is free at restaurants (unless this book becomes wildly successful). This recipe works well with all kinds of bread and is better with bread that is a few days old and hard. So don't worry about that take-out bag that you thought was useless because the bread is now as hard as a rock and could be a weapon. You have the power of your soup pot!

WHAT YOU NEED:

- A loaf or half a loaf of your leftover bread. (you can mix and match)
- 2-3 cans of tomatoes. You can use diced or peeled whole (whichever is on sale)
- 1 quart of chicken broth. (if you don't have it, forget it, your soup will just be thicker)

- 3-5 chopped cloves of garlic
- 1 chopped onion
- red pepper flakes (again, if you like that sort of thing)
- ½ Parmesan cheese.
- 2 Tablespoons of Butter (or half a short stick if you're a butter nut like me)
- Salt and Pepper to taste
- Handful of parsley leaves (you can get these from someone's garden for free or better yet, plant an herb garden yourself!)
- Olive Oil

WHAT YOU DO:

1. Heat up a medium to large pot (depending on how much soup you want) and drizzle in the olive oil. Once it's hot, add the garlic and then the onions and stir like you did in the other recipes. Add the red pepper flakes if you like that sort of thing.

Dash in salt and pepper and add the cans of whatever tomatoes you have.

2. Using a wooden spoon (so you don't scratch your pan) crush up the tomatoes if you used the peeled kind. They will explode so careful that you're not wearing all white. Add the chicken stalk. If you don't have it, use a few cups of water. Add some more salt and pepper. You're about to add bread so it will soak it all up.

3. Break up all that bread with your hands into bite-size chunks and drop it in there. Think of all the old habits you're breaking away from as you do it. If that bread has gotten too hard, you might have to cut it with a knife. Don't use it if it has mold on it for crying out loud! Add everything else. That's your parsley and your cheese.

4. Stir it or toss it gently to try to keep the bread chucks chunky (otherwise it turns into a mush). If you want to be fancy you can serve it with a sprinkle of parsley and cheese on top too.

Yum! Look at you and your bread soup. I'm so proud. Enough recipes. You get the picture.

If you have leftovers like corn, chicken or anything that can be separated, you can put them in small freezer bags and freeze them for later.

Now go back to dating.

CHAPTER 15

GETTING ACTION

(NOT THAT KIND)

YOU'RE DATING, THAT MEANS YOU'RE EATING!

Your first date may have been a tad nerve-wracking. But by the time you've had your third, fourth and fifth dates, you'll get the hang of it. You're eating! And as a

> Remember to Listen!

bonus, if you're *really* listening to your dates while you're eating, you're probably meeting some pretty cool guys. Despite all the horror stories on the news about "dangerous men", there are great guys out there, especially when you're not filled with anxiety about finding Prince Charming.

Where has the search for Prince Charming gotten you anyway? If anything, it has made you hungry! When you remove the goal of romance and just focus on your date for who he is, and not who you're hoping he might be from your childhood fantasies, you will have a damn good time while you're getting your belly filled.

If you're like me, and we've established that you are since you're reading this – you may be wondering if you're a jerk for dating for food.   You're probably wondering if you should just tell your dates straight away and come clean about what you're doing. Maybe you should even just go ahead and pick up the check this one time –to make it all fair to the guys.

STOP THINKING ABOUT IT!
STOP RIGHT NOW!

Let me remind you once again that you need not feel guilty for receiving the gift of food. You are a delightful human being.

Sharing a meal with you in your cute classy outfit and your clean teeth and nails and having you listen attentively during dinner is a wonderful pleasure.

Food is a gift, and YOU are a gift as well. Don't forget that.

You are Breaking a Pattern!

And remember, you are doing this not only to eat, but also to break a pattern of always being the "nice" one that bears the burden, pays the check, and makes sure everyone else is taken care of while you starve. Remember? It's hard at first, isn't it? But it gets easier so keep it up. You can't break a pattern if you go back to your old ways!

If you so much as have a passing thought about picking up the check and "confessing" that you are dating for food, stop yourself, check your issues at the door and just listen, listen, listen to your date.

People love to be listened to and they are *grateful* that someone is actually hearing what they say. Why? Because nobody listens anymore! Everyone is so damn busy tweeting, Facebooking and tab browsing, even at the dinner table with the family, it's a wonder they don't tweet each other to pass the butter!

Listening is a caring, thoughtful gesture - just like feeding someone is a caring, thoughtful gesture. See how it works? So knock off the guilt, OK? Think about it this way. Therapists get paid a lot of money because they take the time to really to listen to people. You're devoting your time and energy doing something similar; it just happens to be during dinner (or lunch or breakfast).

You deserve to be paid, too, so think about being fed as a kind of paycheck. Even though you're not a professional listener, you're becoming highly skilled in the lost art of listening by Dating 4 Food.

If you don't believe me, just watch the people around you the next time you go out, and pay attention to how they listen. Most people are just waiting for others to finish talking so they can share what they have already thought about saying as soon as you stop talking. People are horrible at listening. But not you. You're fantastic at it. You are getting really good at listening because you're spending most of your date doing just that – Listening!

Listening is a Lost Art.

Believe me, the better you are at hearing what your date has to say, the better the food will be. Seriously. If you're a mediocre listener, you'll get mediocre food. Listening is like cash. The more you have to offer, the more you get in return.

If this still doesn't seem fair to you, ask yourself why?

Why is your time not valuable? Why are so many women so quick to see themselves as a burden instead of a valued treasure? If you barely see yourself as worthy, you will be tempted to at least go Dutch, but I beg you not to do this. Just fake it for a few dates and see how easy it will be to accept that a really nice guy thinks you're great, he literally can't stop himself from buying you a fabulous meal! He's too busy talking about himself to think about anything else! You are delightful and wonderful and it is his pleasure to take you out.

Because you are always such a joy to be with, you can go on dates again and again and again. Yes, that's right. It is perfectly acceptable for you to get a lot of action. (not that kind of action!) We're talking good old-fashioned fishing action; real bites, solid catches and yummy vittles.

With practice, you can line up a date for every meal thus keeping yourself fed, and sometimes highly entertained, while you get your life in order.

GO OUT WITH ANYONE

I've said it before in **Rule Number 8**, but it needs repeating: Do not discriminate and reject all the guys you think won't turn out to be marriage material. Go out with anyone (except creeps and weirdoes). When you're hungry you need an active meal plan aka a dating calendar! Don't stop at dinner either, make time for lunch and breakfast too.

Some old guys are in bed by nine anyway so getting your butt out of bed early to have breakfast at the local diner is a fine way to accommodate the older men while filling your belly with food bright and early.

Plus, making sure you eat helps you avoid the shakes (and headaches) from lack of nutrition later in the day. And older guys have amazing stories. Listen up.

Plus, a guy might spring for a cheap lunch on the first date because he wants to see if you're a good person. If you do a good job listening to him and are genuinely interested, he'll likely spring for the more expensive food on the second or third date. Just don't mislead him to believe you're moving in a serious direction if he's not your long-term-guy type.

Be better than I was about discriminating against things like height and age. You'll be better fed. I have a thing about guys who are shorter than me. It annoys me. Plus, they can see my chin hair if I missed plucking one! That's an issue for us tall women, you know.

I could write an entirely different book about chin hair.

Anyway, I once met a very hot guy at a bar (this was before I realized I had to Date 4 Food). He asked for my number and I gave it to him because, what the hell, he was hot. Then he stood up and he was a good foot and a half shorter than I was. I asked for my number back. What a jerk I was. This is exactly the kind of thing you should not do when you are dating for food!

It's critically important that you stop yourself from focusing on the same kind of guy you *think* is your type anyway. Where has that gotten you so far? How much debt did that last one leave you with? Did you try to "help" him with his career? Did you give him a cell phone? A car? Did you pay off his computer? Listen here → **SNAP OUT OF IT!**

If I had a dime for every woman who has supported a starving artist boyfriend or a deadbeat husband, I wouldn't ever have had to date4food. You are not alone. A lot of us have tried to "save" these kinds of guys.

It's okay. Hold yourself and rock back and forth. Pat yourself on the back. You're done with that nonsense. And to celebrate, you are not going to pick up the check - ever! Say it with me "I am never going to pick up the check again". Good girl.

Now, open your mind, and your calendar, and accept the fact that it is perfectly okay for you to get some action. Food action. But it is not okay to discriminate. Trust me, go out with guys you think are not your type, even if they seem like the kind of guy you would never even consider dating, much less marrying. You are going to be pleasantly surprised to learn how wrong you are about what a "good guy" looks like, and you most certainly will change your way of thinking about whether you ever dated the right *type* when you are not stuck with the bill! Bonus. I know, aren't you excited? I'm excited for you.

You might start to feel sorry for yourself for wasting so much time ignoring the interesting guys while your head was stuck up the broke hunk's ass! Sorry, that was harsh but it needed to be said.

I can see you scrolling through the racks of men thinking to yourself "I would

Tell Your Picky Brain to Take a Hike!

never be caught dead going out with that guy". Let me tell you something Prissy Missy - you tell your picky little brain to shut up! When you think you can pick your "type" based on the guy's looks, height, weight, nationality or whatever other excuses you come up with, you are fooling yourself, wasting precious time and money (often on handsome moochers), and missing out on opportunities to spend time with interesting guys who live interesting lives AND are happy to buy YOU a good meal!

And hey, you might meet someone that your best friend or your mom would like to date for real! You will surely meet really cool guys who become *friends*. And though I dare not mention it, in fact ignore what I am about to tell you.

You *might* just meet a guy you really like. That's right, I'm talking about *the one*. It's not your plan - it shouldn't be your focus - but lots of wondrous things happen when you **Date4Food.**

CHAPTER 16
WHEN YOU'RE NOT DATING

GET YOUR LIFE TOGETHER, DUH

When you're not dating or searching for food by putting men into your Hot List, what are you doing? Hopefully you're looking for and getting a job. If you already have a job, you might be exploring ways of working better, harder, faster - or maybe you're going back to school or learning a new talent. This is all great. You don't want to date4food forever. There are too many lazy jerks in this world that never get their own mojo going. Don't be like those lame boobs. Work at becoming your most amazing self while you're Dating for Food. Excel!

You're a Mess. Fix Yourself.

While you are dating for food, do not waste precious time snooping around all the various dating sites. You have too much going on to dawdle in cyberspace.

The Internet can be a time vampire. Do not let it suck the life out of you. Instead, use it to help you build your fabulous life. Dedicate at least two hours a day to your various social media sites. If you're the type who hates Facebook, get over yourself. It is your future whether you like it or not. Saying you don't like Facebook is like saying you don't want to use your phone because you'd rather ride a horse to deliver a message. (Not that I don't love a good ride but we're talking about communication technology not equestrian leisure activities.) You can use sites like Facebook to Date 4 Food too, you know.

On the other hand, if you're the type who spends most of your day on social media sites, get off your ass, unplug yourself and get some fresh air.

When **dating4food**, you don't want to be seen as the kind of gal whose social life begins and ends on her laptop on her sofa. If you have trouble getting dates, it won't be because you haven't spent enough time searching. It will be because you have not opened your mind enough to consider the kind of guy that might not seem your type. Trust me. You need to stop busying yourself with new searches on new sites in the hope some shirtless hunk will message you.

Take the hunky guys off your Hotlist and stop reposting them twenty times so that their profiles ping constantly with your profile headline. All that effort is a total waste of time because, guess what, those guys aren't real. OK maybe a few of them are real, but most are spam robots. That's right - spam robots.

Don't Waste Time on Robots.

Some tech-punk strategically dumped them into your dating site because he knew you'd be looking for exactly that "type" and if you click on it and share your email, guess what? You'll start getting spammed. Yet another reason to avoid the hunks.

Don't try to date a spam robot! Even if a few of them are actual guys, remember that the hunky ones will only want to meet for drinks and will try to get YOU to pick up the tab. Bottom line - I will repeat this again - ignore the hotties.

If you ignore the hunks and you're still not getting food dates, you're being too picky. Answer all messages from guys aged 18-80. Hell, don't stop at 80. If he's ninety and wants to buy you a pot roast, let him! When you're not dating, shoot some new pictures of yourself to post to show how interesting you are. Go places and actually DO interesting things and then write about it on your dating profile.

Ride your bike, attend a free lecture at a local university, visit a museum using passes you can get from your local library, take a walk in a beautiful setting (all of these things are free, by the way) and share *short sweet* stories on your profile about how active and cool you are. You're awesome but guys won't know this about you unless you make yourself interesting in your profile. Don't overdo it about yourself though, because Super Woman stuff can scare a guy away.

It's better to say you ran six miles or went on a bike ride around the city than talking about climbing Mount Kilimanjaro, giving blood and saving baby seals - all in one day! And for heaven's sake - don't lie. If you only ran a city block, don't say you ran a 10K. Just like if you are shaped like a potato, don't say you model on the side.

You're perfect just the way you are.

Go to a Co-Dependents (CODA) anonymous meeting and listen to how many other people have had your problem. You're not the only one, right? I told you. Hearing stories from others about how they always paid the check, lost their house, gave their car to their ex only to have him run off with it, took in every single homeless three-legged animal in the neighborhood, and made sure everyone they ever met had their absolute full attention and any money in their wallet will make you feel like less of a loser. A few meetings can't hurt. Try it.

They are FREE!

You can find meetings in your area at coda.org. Why don't you go find one now? I'll wait.

Set a Budget

Dating4food will save you lots of money. Want to know how much? How much do you usually spend on groceries and going out? Every Date 4 Food

Don't Be Afraid of Budgets.

reduces your grocery and "entertainment" expenses, especially when you take home leftovers! Think about how much you are saving every time you decide whether to answer a message from a guy that doesn't seem like your "type". When you don't message a potential date back, you're basically choosing not to cut your expenses.

I made a bad habit out of eating out in Los Angeles and New York City, which meant that one night out could easily cost me fifty bucks for the cheapest place, not including gas, subway or taxi costs.

It was often closer to a hundred bucks, and then when I offered to pay for everyone else like an idiot, I had a very hefty bill in front of me at the end of the night.

How many times have you done that? After you date4food for a while, picking up the tab for everyone else doesn't make sense anymore. The way I looked at it, I could pay for my cell phone and Internet bill with the money I saved while Dating 4 Food. And because I stopped paying for others, I could afford bigger things like getting my car fixed!

Isn't this fun? It's even more delightful when you realize you have enough money leftover every month to pay down your debt and ideally start a new savings account. You can do this for free online. Try IngDirect.com and tell them I sent you. Fight the urge to spend the money you're saving. All of these lessons I'm sharing with you will all be for naught if go back to your old ways after Dating4Food.

Make an Excel spreadsheet of all of your monthly bills and include a provision that measures the payments you are making to reduce your debts. You will be amazed to watch your savings grow and to see how much money you DON'T spend on men you're dating (or have sleeping for free on your sofa!).

You might not consider yourself an investor who understands the Stock Market but read magazines about money management. They always have tips for people who don't spend a lot of time on Wall Street.

Better yet, read a Suze Orman book, or even better, watch her FREE videos on YouTube. She has easy-to-understand tips about saving money that even I could take advantage of (though she doesn't suggest dating4food so maybe she could learn a thing or two from me!).

Cut loose extra charges &
Charge Extra

I'm not suggesting you evict the ex-boyfriend who's sleeping on your couch and paying his share of rent. Keep all the decent sharers-of-rent around. If you have people eating from your leftover recipes put a box in the kitchen with a slit in the top that says "Nobody Eats For Free" and charge everyone five bucks to eat at your house. Believe me, it's cheaper for them to do that than to go out. Plus, the usually get a kick out of it, especially when you give them your best "I'm dead serious" look. Take that food money and put it in your savings account.

Then cut loose all the charges that you forgot about that are attached directly to your bank debit card or any of your credit cards. You can't do this until you go through your statements to see what the hell I'm talking about.

Look through all of your statements while your Co-Dependent Casserole is cooking. Comb through every charge you see. For example, did you upgrade your Netflix account to Blu-ray but you can't even play Blu-ray disks because you had to sell your Blu-ray player for beans and rice?

Downgrade your account. In fact, find a way to watch movies online for free until you're out of debt. Go to Hulu. Blockbuster.com also has a list of free movies and so does Amazon if you have Amazon Prime. You can upgrade to Amazon Prime if you've been on so many dates and that you've saved enough to get it.

Cancel anything and everything that costs you money. If you broke **Rule Number 5** and upgraded your online dating account to Gold, cancel it immediately. Don't be a sucker for the online vultures. Take control of your messy life. It has to be done.

ReRead the Rules!

While you're at it, get rid of the crap the last starving artist left in your house and take it all to Goodwill. Get a tax write-off. If you're broke and have no income you don't need a write-off, but by dumping the junk you'll be psychologically even better prepared to open your mind to other types of men as you continue your Dating 4 Food. By the way, I wrote Will Date 4 Food with the number 4 because I was four months late on my bills. You feel my pain. But by setting a budget and going out with anyone I was able to get back on schedule and get my bills paid. You will be too!

MAKE A VISION BOARD

It's time to envision your life so that you no longer live the caretaker Mama Warbucks role as the savior of all losers.

Try to imagine what your house would look like if it were set up the way you like it and not as a bunker for the needy guys in the band?

Have you ever made a vision board? If you watch Oprah or any of the self-help gurus, you've probably heard of them. It's a collage of images and words that mean something to you. Vision boards are fun and easy to do. Buy a piece of poster board at the 99 Cent store, along with a glue stick. Grab some old magazines, newspapers, fliers etc. from friends and doctors' offices.

Look through all sorts of magazines and find images that give you a good feeling about your life. Choose pictures of strong and successful women. Find anything that means abundance to you and put it on your vision board.

Vision Boards are Fun.

Sometimes you have to imagine a life that you don't really know yet or may have never known before, but as the saying goes "if you build it, they will come". Build your vision board to reflect the life you have dreamed about; but leave out the things that represent you saving the world and everyone in it.

Your vision board is about **you** and what you love and want and feel passionate about. It's empowering to see your hopes and dreams on a vision board. It's also a great way to learn about yourself when you have to choose images that make you feel a certain way about life. Plus, playing around with scissors and glue sticks is always fun.

Hang your vision board somewhere in your house where you are certain to see it every single day. I hung mine on the ceiling above my bed so I would stare up at it as I fell asleep and it was the first thing I would see in the morning.

And guess what? Everything on that board is in my life now. When we imagine the life we want and then set out to live it - it actually happens. Dating 4 Food is part of getting yourself to that life you really want because it exposes you to new ways of thinking about relationships while saving you money as you chart your new life course.

CHAPTER 17
WEIRDOES, FREAKS & CREEPS

DON'T BE SHARK BAIT

Remember in Chapters 6 and 7 I told you about ignoring the bobbers and deleting the sharks? Well, sometimes, though it's rare, you meet a weirdo, a freak or a creep in person who makes the bobber seem downright charming. These guys are scary and should be avoided at all costs.

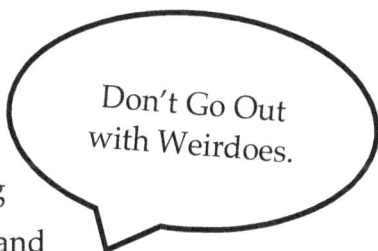

Don't Go Out with Weirdoes.

You can avoid weirdoes, freaks and creeps most of the time just by reading their profiles carefully. They usually give themselves away.

Like the guy who started having message fights with me as if we'd been dating for years and I'd never even met him before! Definite freak. Then there was the guy who started texting me every day about how our astrology signs were aligned and he wanted to feel my chakras. Yikes. Weirdo. Or of course the guy in Santa Monica in the sweater. Creep. Don't risk meeting those types of guys in person. No meal is worth your safety and you have better things to do than put up with even a non-dangerous whack-job no matter how good the food!

Warning signs are not always clear but trust your gut. If your womanly sense is on edge when you read his dinner invite, don't go! And if you get there and the hair on your skin is standing straight up get out of there. This is when your Dating Buddy aka The Gay Mafia that we learned about in Chapter 3 comes in handy.

Weirdoes and Freaks can be just that – weird and freaky. I went on a date with one guy who cried the whole time. I couldn't even ask questions to get him to talk about himself because he wouldn't stop crying. It was very odd, although I did get a great sandwich and excellent bowl of soup out of the deal!

Another guy started telling me how he

Watch Out for Ass-Droids!

was afraid of being hit by an asteroid. The horror of random asteroids plummeting to Earth plagued his days and nights. Wow. I kept with the Dating4Food protocol and asked questions like "when do you think an asteroid is going to hit?" I hoped it wasn't during dinner because even though the guy was beyond strange, the meal was scrumptious.

Weirdoes are easy to spot, too, because they ask weird questions.

They speak in code or message you in all CAPS, telling you the problems they think you'll have in your future relationship together. There are exceptions to the "Avoid All Caps" rule. My mother met the best guy in her life online dating. She didn't respond to him at first since he wrote her in all caps! But it turned out his caps lock was broken. He is now feeding her regularly and they are having great senior sex too, but that's an entirely different book.

Weirdoes have odd beliefs and hobbies that you will have to Google just to know what they're talking about. One guy sent me a daily message about how horrified he was that we were breaking up. I considered sending a reply that said, "dude, we've never met", but I blocked him instead. Another guy barely got past message number one when he started telling me how his wife left him after he drove their car through the garage, drunk and high on pain meds.

That guy then told me how he'd tried to kill himself after that and wanted to know if I would go to an NA (Narcotics Anonymous) meeting with him later that night. Unbelievable. Even if they served filet mignon at the meeting, this is not a guy anyone should date for food or anything else. He needed professional help, not a date.

Weirdoes and freaks are usually harmless, and hey, they gave me some great fodder for this book. But don't take chances. Get out of the restaurant as fast as you can and never, I repeat never, date him a second time. Save your repeat dates for the good guys. I don't care how hungry you are.

Eat your leftovers, eat your front lawn or hit up your girlfriends who are Dating4Food for their leftovers for a few days. Just do NOT go on a second date with a weirdo or a freak.

Some freaky guys are just angry. They don't have paranoia and they don't cry, but they're creepy because they're very, very angry. These are also men to be avoided no matter what they buy you for dinner.

I agreed to a date with an angry guy once. He didn't seem angry in his profile. In fact, he wrote that he was a vegan. How could he be angry, I thought. Vegans eat the kind of stuff that cleans your colon and should make you less of an ass than the ordinary constipated jerk. But not this guy. He had a weird green chip on his shoulder, like everyone who was NOT a vegan was toxic and should be destroyed. After we ate our delicious ruffage, the check came and we both stared at it. Then we drank our jasmine tea and waited for the other one to get the check. He must have read the same book I read where it says that whoever touches the check first pays the bill.

We sat there until the place closed. Literally, the owner came out himself and turned the Open sign on the door to Closed. Hint. Then the owner started mopping around us. I'm not kidding. In the end, we went Dutch. Yes, I broke a rule and it was a hard one too since I had already done what I told you to do in Chapter 16 – *When You're Not Dating.* I had spent the week creating a great budget for myself and that dinner was not on the list. Raw food is pricey too. I don't get that. I'm sorry; I tried to be a Vegetarian once, a Vegan another time and even spent a spell as a Macrobiotic. In the end, I am a Southern girl. I eat meat. Plus, it turned out that I was allergic to soy. That was not good on those diets. You can pay outrageous prices for a raw food dish if you want to. If I'm paying, I'm getting the bargain-priced chicken potpie.

Even Vegans Can be Weird.

That was just a little story to remind you that weirdoes can be packaged to look good on the outside. It's also a friendly reminder that even though you should plan never to go Dutch, especially with a weirdo, you may have to if you don't want to sit all night in a restaurant with angry Vegan. Some things are worse than going Dutch!

YOUR GREAT EXIT

Getting away from weirdoes is relatively easy, unless you have a real creep on your hands and have to resort to using a weapon (not a gun, silly, the Gay Mafia. Reread Chapter 3 – *Your Dating Buddy aka The Gay Mafia*). If you can't shake a weirdo by eating fast and flying home because he insists on having dessert somewhere else, or going to hear a band playing at such-and-such place, it's time to play dirty.

This is when you can start talking about your issues. (Re-read Chapter 12 – *Check Your Issues with the Valet* and do everything I told you not to do). Stop listening to him. Go on and on about yourself and all of your problems; in fact, create a few problems to make yourself seem even more troubled than you really are. There's no better buzz-kill than a crazy woman going off on her never ending list of issues with men, money and mental health. Of course, don't do any of this until AFTER he has paid the check. Trust me, there will be no after-party. He will be out of there in a flash.

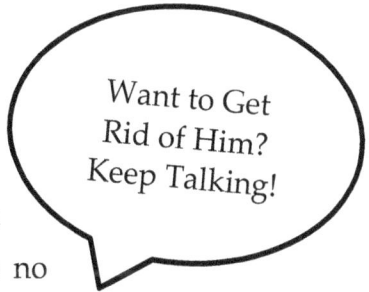

Here are some other ways to get out of a bad date quickly or inspire him to make a run for it fast.

→ Your ailing grandmother is living with you and you have to get home to change her diapers.

IF THAT DOESN'T SCARE HIM AWAY, TRY THESE:

→ You have to get up early to get your seven kids off to school.

→ Your ex-husband is getting out of prison tomorrow and he's coming to pick you up.

→ You just peed on yourself.

→ Ask him if he would consider marrying you before the end of the year, because it would help with your probation status.

→ Tell him you spoke to your mother and she's expecting both of you for lunch tomorrow. Tell him she lives in a small trailer by the river.

→ Tell him you posted his picture from the dating site on your Facebook page and wrote that he's your new boyfriend.

→ Tell him you have period cramps.

If none of the above work, here is the mother load:

I have diarrhea.

No guy is going urge you to stay. In fact, he will help you leave. You can add that you get the runs weekly and really have to rush home. Don't worry; you will probably never see him again.

CHAPTER 18
REPEAT BITES

NOTHING LIKE A REPEAT DATE!

If you get asked out again, go! Even if you don't really like him and

Accept Every Offer for a Repeat Date!

don't want to be seen with him, stop being a snobby fuddy-duddy and go. I went on the most dates with a man I called CEO Guy. He was not a guy I would have ever pictured myself with romantically, but he had spectacular taste in food and wine. He was also very entertaining and smart so I loved talking to him and I learned a lot of stuff about the business world. You know why? Because I listened to him!

The more I listened, the more I learned. He taught me about wines, too, and cool things like where to find the best and least expensive food in New York City. He was better than Yelp and Zagat. I was getting knowledge and great food - for free!

You don't have to limit yourself to the area near where you live or work. You can date for food wherever you go. When I was scheduled to fly to New York for business while living in LA, I simply switched my location on my dating profile from Los Angeles to New York and voila – dinner plans. It's harder to have repeat dates in places where you don't live, but keep the guy's contact information in case you return.

Repeat dates are also great practice for when you meet someone you think you might *really* like. You can literally practice your listening skills while learning about yourself because you get to figure out what it is that makes a guy interesting to *you*.

On repeat dates, you can talk a bit more about yourself because any guy who wants to keep feeding you obviously wants to hear more about why you're such a delightful person. This is helpful for when you meet that special someone because you're practicing being yourself! That sounds weird, I know. But so many women spend time trying to act like they're someone they're not. They don't even know how to be themselves when it comes to having a healthy relationship with someone who's truly interested in them for who they are. Think of it this way. Dating4food is an inexpensive and delicious way for you to practice relating to men. By the time you get your skill-set in place, you'll be so desirable, men will be lined up in cyber-space begging to buy you dinner!

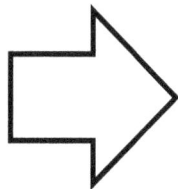

TRY NEW FOOD

When you're asked out for a repeat date – try a new

> Open Your Mind & Your Palate!

place! Branch out. Open your mind and your palate. And if he asks about your palate, don't say something dumb like I once did to a dentist who told me I needed tissue removed from my palate. I almost fainted at the idea of my dentist performing stomach surgery. I know, I was an idiot. If you don't know what a palate is (or some other word comes up at a restaurant where lots of the menu items are not written in English) ASK! A guy loves to be the smart one who teaches his date a thing or two about the coq au vin. Rather than risking sounding like a dope, ask questions.

This way you will sound curious rather than dopey and he gets to sound smart, which strokes his ego. Win-win all around. And don't assume all the smart guys are dressed in suits!

I met a date4food once at an awesome barbeque place. The guy showed up in overalls. You might have thought he looked weird but I'm a Southern girl, I thought it was awesome. During dinner, he pulled three bottles of BBQ sauce out of his bag. He traveled with his own sauce! When I asked him about it, he gave me a full history of the little place in South Carolina that made the sauce. He stocked up every time he visited. It was an awesome date and Barbecue Man was super smart so keep your stereotypes in check when dating4food.

Note that you shouldn't always jump at the chance to eat something from a jar your date brings to the restaurant. It could be laced with a drug or unsafe for other reasons.

Think about the situation and err on the side of caution. I knew a lot of people who knew this guy and we had a lot of mutual Facebook friends so I tried it and it was worth it. Not only was he a very cool guy, but that BBQ sauce of his was the best I ever had! He was a great guy with great sauce. He would have been perfect for one of my aunts.

Having an open mind means trying new things, from the food to the men. Barbecue Man was not someone I would have ordinarily considered dating. But guess what? We're still Facebook friends and I will never forget him or his unbelievable sauce!

CHAPTER 19
FISHING FOR FRIENDS

IS YOUR DATE A FRIEND'S FUTURE HUSBAND?

Dating4food is about so much more than just food! You're essentially

You Date Could Become a Friend!

forcing yourself to meet people you would never otherwise have had a chance to know. This is a good thing because some of the guys you go out with will become friends for life.

Even if the guys are not your type, they might make great mates for your friends, but you'll only find these guys if you strictly follow **Rule Number 8:** *Go out with anyone who asks (minus weirdoes, freaks and creeps).*

When you date a guy with the potential to become a serious relationship for a friend, make sure to have your friend show up, oops, while you're on your date! Be sure it's at the end of the date and you've had your fill of dinner. Remember, you're the one dating4food here! Your pal can show up for dessert or an after dinner drink. Call her when you go to the bathroom, right after you order your cheesecake.

DON'T TEXT AT THE TABLE

I thought my friend Kat would like Mr. CEO Guy. He was really interesting and, just like Kat, had great taste in food, clothes and nice cars. I was intrigued to learn about those things from the guy, but all that fancy stuff wasn't really my style. I like a guy who's good with a chainsaw, can bring in the firewood and build me a house. But most of all, I like sexy geeks. But Mr. CEO guy was a whole other cut of beef.

I called my friend Kat during a bathroom visit during a date with Mr. CEO and told her to get her cute little fanny down there pronto. I added that she should show a little cleavage and put some gloss on her lips. Duh.

She could break the rules and come in looking sexy. She wasn't dating for food, I was! Kat met us after dinner at the bar. CEO Guy loved it. It was like a twofer for him. He even bought her a dessert and two glasses of amazing wine. They went out separately after that, which is the only drawback of hooking up your friends with your dates. Your meals dry up! If you do lose a repeat date to a good friend, make sure she knows that you expect her to at least bring you leftovers from HER dates with the guy! You can show her how to make your favorite Co-Dependent casserole recipe.

CHAPTER 20
THE BEST CATCH EVER

THIS IS NOT JUST ABOUT FOOD

If you haven't figured this out by now, *Will Date 4 Food* is a self-help book. Yes it is. Reread it and you'll see. You're not just going on dates to get men to buy you food. You're bettering yourself! You're learning to listen. You're becoming empowered. And guess what? You're saving money, too, because you never picked up the check! Not once. (Except for Dutch incidents when desperate. You are forgiven.)

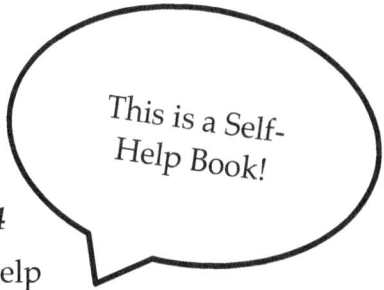

Have you noticed how the more dates you have, the more comfortable you've become not picking up the tab?

This is a Self-Help Book!

Do you see that it's perfectly all right for someone else to take you to dinner? Have you calculated how much you've saved so far? It's great, isn't it?

HOW MUCH HAVE YOU SAVED?

While you're pondering how much money you've saved, don't forget that it's because you deserved all those good meals. You were a good a good listener and you put all that effort into making sure you got all dressed up like you were going to job interview at Google.

Now would be a good time to pay your accountant. He or she has probably been yelling at you for spending all your money treating everyone else, and now you're moving in the direction of taking care of yourself. You should be proud of yourself. Now it's a good idea to pay your accountant. If you don't have one, get one.

If you have an accountant, and you're lucky like me, then he or she has been really patient with you and maybe "forgot" to send you bills while you were struggling. Take some of what you've saved dating4food and say thank with a little payment. Then start paying off the rest of your debts. For every hundred dollars you pay down on

Debt is SO Dated. Get Out of It!

your debt, you'll be another ten percent happier. Debt is depressing.

When your debt is finally under control, you will be very happy. In fact, you will want to write love songs about **Will Date 4 Food** because you will be eating better, meeting good guys **and** have your finances in order! But don't bother with a love song. An Amazon testimonial will suffice. We want other women to get in on the delicious cost-saving action, too.

With more money in your pocket, you might want to give handouts to the next starving artist who shows up but don't be tempted! Even though Soap Star was horribly annoying, he was right about debt. I never even thought of debt with such disdain until I went out with that narcissist.

Bless their hearts; I learned something from almost every date I went on, just like you'll learn a lot of things from Dates 4 Food, even if they are jerks.

By focusing on things like getting out of debt, I learned to look at all sorts of things in my life differently, and I started noticing patterns in my life that were unhealthy for my body *and* my bank account. As soon as I started taking care of my needs, by doing things like **dating4food**, my life turned around. If things start going well for you, too, after reading this book, please buy another copy and send it to a friend. Then I'll be doing even better!

CHANGE THE WAY YOU DATE

Date 4 Food tips will work well even if you find a guy you're serious about. The only thing to knock off the list if you meet a love interest is **Rule Number 8.** You can't rightly date a pile of guys, for food or anything else, while you're making nice with Mr. Right.

Good Men Exist! Tell Your Friends!

Good Men Exist! They're everywhere but women have unfortunately been trained to look for bums and jerks. **Will Date 4 Food** is all about retraining your brain to notice and listen to good guys. Learning to take the time to know all types of men will make it easier to notice real love when it shows up.

I met the man of my dreams after **dating4food**. He's a guy I might never have found if I hadn't changed the way I think about men and stopped my pattern of supporting the starving artist boys. He's a sexy geek who also happens to be great with a chainsaw too. Score! If I hadn't dated guys outside of my usual pattern I might not have seen how wonderful my man truly is. By the way, he's tall, too; six-foot-four to be exact. Best of all, besides the fact that he's the most amazing man I've ever met; he doesn't cost me a dime.

Meeting a good guy you're romantically interested in, or who becomes your boyfriend or husband does not mean you have to start picking up the check! Duh. Keep your finances and your wallet to yourself even if you meet the love of your life. You can pay for the baby diapers or the new wallpaper. You'll work out finances if you end up committed or married to the guy. Between now and when the wedding bells ring, practice the Dating 4 Food Rules with all date-worthy guys at all times.

THOUGHTS TO DIGEST

It has been a pleasure to share all of this valuable information with you. I'm sorry you needed this book in the first place, but again, you are not alone! I want to you remember that you are awesome and a wonderful dinner partner (when you check yourself and behave).

Just because you got yourself into a predicament by taking care of everyone else, it doesn't mean that you are any less adorable. In fact, it is the usually the amazing people who put their hearts and wallets on the line for others. But if you've learned one thing from me I hope it is that you do not have to take care of everyone else. They can take care of themselves. You make sure your life is in order, that you are out of debt and that you have money in your savings account before you start even thinking about giving anything away.

Hopefully you have moved beyond those old patterns and supporting starving artist boyfriends is far in your past. Now that you've learned all the benefits of Dating for Food, get out there and get yourself fed. Hit me up on Facebook and let me know which parts of the book worked best for you. If you have any recipes to add to the list, send them to me and I'll post them on the website.

Best of all, take care of yourself. You're worth it. You're sweet, pretty and just perfect the way you are. May you be well fed.

VISIT

WILLDATE4FOOD.COM

FACEBOOK US @

FACEBOOK.COM/WILLDATEFORFOOD

ACKNOWLEDGEMENTS

Thank you to all my Facebook friends who are active on my wall. Thank you to the many men who fed me while I was dating for food. I'm sorry I didn't tell you what I was doing. I'm not mentioning any names.

Thank you Ali Drummond for sending me groceries when I was starving and didn't have a date. God Bless Shawn Caulin Young for all that he does in my life, including cleaning that mess from my plumbing exploding while I was on a date. Thank you Jennifer Welker for making my visions into a reality with your great designs.

Many thanks to Kelly McCormick and Marci Liroff for sitting me down and telling me I had a problem supporting man boys. Much love to my family for reading the first drafts and feeding me during the process.

Many thanks to my manager, Sheree Guitar, who says I will never fit into a box and should quit trying. I'm grateful that she thinks the comedy script based on this book is hilarious.

If we make any money on the movie, I promise to not spend it on boys (unless I have a son). Thank you to Wendy Murphy for being a ruthless reader and good friend of mine.

Thank you to Elliot Titleman at Quiet Owl Books. Bless your big brain for being able to see that I can write a humorous how-to book one day and a children's book and a mystery the next. It's always a bonus to know people who 'see' me.

Best of all, thank you to the man I love. I'm so glad you can cook.

RIP THESE PAGES OUT AND KEEP THEM IN YOUR WALLET

RULES FOR WILL DATE 4 FOOD!

RULE NUMBER 1: Never have anyone pick you up at your house. Meet your dates at a mutually agreeable establishment. More than everything else, you need to be safe which means not letting your date know where you live.

RULE NUMBER 2: Have a Dating Buddy aka the Gay Mafia. This is who knows where you're going and whom you are going out with and even better than that, drops you off and picks you up.

RULE NUMBER 3: Do not meet for drinks or coffee. The whole point is to eat real food not bar snacks.

RULE NUMBER 4: Do not focus on romance. Focus on the food. (If love shows up, that's a great extra helping, not the goal.)

RULE NUMBER 5: Do not upgrade your online dating account or spend any money on dating sites.

RULE NUMBER 6: Do not pick up the check (duh) even to "go Dutch". You are not allowed to pay. Remember, you're dating for food.

RULE NUMBER 7: Listen Listen Listen. Let him talk while you eat. Bet you never did that before.

RULE NUMBER 8: Go out with anyone who asks (minus weirdoes, freaks and creeps).

RULE NUMBER 9: Check your issues with the valet and hold your tongue. This is no time to treat your date like he's your therapist. You can't have a free mean and a free counseling session.

RULE NUMBER 10: Eat Well. Do not order just a salad. Go for sustenance.

If you feel compelled to pick up the check – STOP yourself. Pick up the Rules instead.

Once I set up a new retirement fund for myself, a portion of the sales from this book will be donated to:

No Kid Hungry
nokidhungry.org

Visit

WILLDATE4FOOD.COM

FACEBOOK US @

FACEBOOK.COM/WILLDATEFORFOOD

Will Date 4 Food

www.ingramcontent.com/pod-product-compliance
Lightning Source LLC
Chambersburg PA
CBHW051824040426
42447CB00006B/355